Jaime J. Sucher

Cocker Spaniels

Everything About Purchase, Care,
Nutrition, Breeding, Behavior, and Training

With a Special Chapter on Understanding
Cocker Spaniels

With 28 Color Photographs
Drawings by Michele Earle-Bridges

Consulting Editor: Matthew M. Vriends, Ph.D.

BARRON'S

About the Author:
Jaime J. Sucher is Director of Research and Development for a manufacturer of pet products. He is the author of *Golden Retrievers*, *Shetland Sheepdogs*, and numerous articles on pet nutrition.

All inquiries should be addressed to:
Barron's Educational Series, Inc.
250 Wireless Boulevard
Hauppauge, New York 11788

International Standard Book No. 0-8120-1478-2

Library of Congress Catalog Card No. 92-38560

Library of Congress Cataloging-in-Publication Data

Sucher, Jaime J.
    Cocker spaniels : everything about purchase, care, nutrition, breeding, behavior, and training : with a special chapter on understanding cocker spaniels / Jaime J. Sucher ; drawings by Michele Earle-Bridges ; consulting editor, Matthew M. Vriends.
        p.   cm. -- (A Complete pet owner's manual)
    Includes bibliographical references (p.   ) and index.
    ISBN 0-8120-1478-2
    1. Cocker spaniels.   I. Vriends, Matthew M., 1937–   II. Title.   III. Series.
SF429.C55S83   1993
636.7'52--dc20   92-38560
                                            CIP

PRINTED IN HONG KONG
3456   9955   987654321

Photo Credits:
Michele Earle-Bridges: page 10, back cover (top left); Gary W. Ellis: front cover, pages 9 (bottom left), 27 (top right and bottom), 45, 46 (bottom), 63 (top right and bottom), 64 (top), back cover (top right and bottom left); Judith E. Strom: pages 9 (top), 27 (top right), 28, 46 (top), 63 (top left), 64 (bottom), back cover (bottom right).

Advice and Warning:
This book is concerned with selecting, keeping, and raising cocker spaniels. The publisher and the author think it is important to point out that the advice and information for cocker spaniel maintenance applies to healthy, normally developed animals. Anyone who acquires an adult dog or one from an animal shelter must consider that the animal may have behavioral problems and may, for example, bite without any visible provocation. Such anxiety-biters are dangerous for the owner as well as the general public.

Caution is further advised in the association of children with dogs, in meetings with other dogs, and in exercising the dog without a leash.

Contents

Contents

Preface

Since you are reading this book, it is logical to assume that you have or are considering the purchase of a cocker spaniel. If you are considering purchase, I urge you to become completely familiar with the breed and its needs, especially if you have never owned a dog before. While owning and caring for a dog can be one of the great experiences of a lifetime, selecting the wrong breed or misjudging your ability to care for a pet will only create disappointment for both you and the dog.

It is generally conceded that, as a family, spaniels originated in Spain—hence the name "spaniel." However, it was not until the breed was introduced into England that the modern-day cocker spaniel began to take shape. The cocker, or "cocking" spaniel, got its name from its proficiency at hunting woodcock. Although the cocker spaniel's inherent desire to hunt renders it a capable "gundog" when thoroughly trained, it is not hunting ability that has led to the breed's popularity.

The cocker has made its greatest mark as a pet and companion animal. This breed is a great lover of home and family, and its relatively small size, even temperament, and devout loyalty to its master allow it to adapt to almost any environment. The cocker is a trustworthy, merry, and loving dog that is in its element when it has a child to play with.

Another factor responsible for making this dog a national favorite is its beauty, which is enhanced by the many color variations found within the breed. Solid black, red or tan, and mixed black and white, black and tan, and occasionally liver and white, are some of the available color schemes.

Its long history, as well as its physical and behavioral characteristics, makes the cocker spaniel truly unique and well worthy of the attention it receives. There was a time, however, when the popularity of this breed almost caused its downfall. During the late 1930s, when people were just beginning to recover from the Great Depression, some Americans found themselves with more money than they had ever known. However, there was still an extreme shortage of goods on which to spend it. Strangely enough, the public then took a fancy to buying puppies, and the cocker was at the top of the list.

When demand exceeded supply, certain people, motivated only by the desire for profit, began to breed any male and female cockers that were available. The result was litters of wetting, biting, and cringing cockers that almost ruined the integrity of the breed. Although this situation took a long time to correct, today's breed has returned to normal appearance and temperament.

This manual is intended for both the novice and the experienced dog owner. It contains practical information on how to choose and raise a cocker spaniel, whether a puppy or an adult dog. There is detailed information on how to care for a new puppy, grooming, housing and supplies, nutrition, and the causes and treatments of various diseases and injuries.

The first chapter covers the history of the cocker spaniel, and another is devoted entirely to training your pet. The first-time dog owner will find detailed information on the fundamentals of instruction that are important in developing a sound training program. Experienced owners may also pick up some useful techniques to make their training sessions a little easier.

Anyone interested in breeding and showing cockers will find valuable tips on choosing a mate, whelping, and the care of newborn puppies, as well as information on the various types of competitions, trials, and tests.

The final chapter is devoted entirely to helping you understand your cocker spaniel. Included are ways to facilitate the dog's adjustment to other family members and to establish the best relationship between you, the master, and your devoted four-legged companion.

I would like to acknowledge the assistance of Dr. Matthew M. Vriends, consulting editor of this series; Helgard Niewisch, D.V.M., who read the manuscript and made invaluable suggestions; and Don Reis and the staff at Barron's.

What Is a Cocker Spaniel?

Humans and Dogs

Dogs have always been considered the first domesticated animals. The actual domestication process of dogs, however, is very hard to trace because it is impossible for archaeologists to distinguish tame wolves from early domestic dogs. Nevertheless, the earliest indisputable records of "dog" remains, discovered at several Middle East sites, date back some 12,000 years. Other evidence of domesticated dogs, found around the world, goes back between 7,000 and 11,500 years. Since 6500 B.C., the dog has existed virtually everywhere alongside prehistoric and modern humans.

The relationship that began with taming the wolf most likely came about as a result of the hunting and scavenging practices of both humans and wolves. Wolves probably started attaching themselves to camps of human hunters, scavenging meals wherever they could. It is also possible that humans learned group hunting techniques by observing how the wolf pack hunts.

Another key to understanding the domestication process is the similarity in the social structure and communication patterns of prehistoric humans and wolves. Primitive people hunted as a group, wolves as a pack; in each case, the individual's bounty was shared with other members of its small society. Likewise, both species communicated not with words, but with facial expressions and body postures. These similarities probably led to an almost mutual understanding between human and wolf.

At first, people probably killed any wolf that ventured too close to their camps. However, in time the humans could provide enough food for both themselves and their attached pack of wolves. Eventually the newborn wolf pups began to rely upon their human "masters" for food, and later for shelter.

While the exact time sequences are unknown, over the next 10,000 years people began to take control of the breeding practices of their "dogs."

Particular characteristics were chosen for inbreeding, and as a result the variations between the different types of dogs became more pronounced. The larger and more aggressive animals may have been bred together to create a progeny of "watchdogs." The more placid or submissive animals may have been mated to supply dogs that would aid in locating and stalking game.

By the first century A.D. the Romans had written records that contain advice on breeding dogs. One such record, by an agricultural authority, suggests breeding animals of "ample size and loud and sonorous bark" to create the best guard dogs. Breeding white dogs results in better sheepdogs "because it [a white dog] is unlike the wild beast" in color, making it easy for both sheep and shepherd to distinguish friend from foe.

The Romans classified dogs into six different groups: house guardian dogs, shepherd dogs, sporting dogs, fighting or war dogs, dogs that ran by scent, and swift dogs which ran by sight. Most modern dogs have ancestors from one or more of these six classifications. It is unlikely, however, that any modern breed resembles the dogs of ancient Rome. Over the centuries, crossbreeding (mating two dogs of different species) prevented many dogs from developing into pure breeds, but this practice did increase the variety of dog types. Only within the past 100 years, however, has the growing knowledge of genetics allowed us to increase the diversity of breeds while establishing pure bloodlines at the same time. Nevertheless, despite the differences in appearance and temperament, all of the modern breeds of dogs still possess many basic instincts that humans were never able to breed out of the wolf.

Origins and Early History of the Cocker Spaniel

The spaniel comprises a very large family of dogs and has a long history. While the dog's exact

What Is a Cocker Spaniel?

origins are unknown, a "spaynel" or "spanyell" is mentioned in some writings of the fourteenth century. Although also found in France and Switzerland, spaniels are commonly believed to have originated in Spain. The earliest drawings of these dogs make them look more like unkempt setters. They appear taller and rangier than our modern spaniels, with short ears and full-length, feathered tails.

It was not until their introduction into England that most of the spaniel breeds we know today began to take shape. The English breeders mated these dogs rather indiscriminately at first, with the size of the dog being the only criterion for selection. The initial step in the separation of breeds was to divide the animals into land spaniels and water spaniels. The large, curly coated dogs were placed in the water spaniel group, while all of the rest were considered land spaniels. Later, the land spaniels were further separated into groups, with size again being the only criterion.

Today there are ten spaniel breeds in the sporting dog group: American water, Brittany, clumber, cocker, English cocker, English springer, field, Irish water, Sussex, and Welsh springer. While the water spaniel and the Brittany are believed to be the result of crossbreeding spaniels with other dog species, all of the others are the result of selective breeding strictly within the spaniel family.

In the early 1800s, two types of English spaniels gained rapidly in popularity. One was the liver and white "springing spaniel," obviously the ancestor of today's modern English springer spaniel. The other was, as one breeder wrote, "smaller with a more curly type of coat and feathering, and diverse in color." This dog became known as the "cocking spaniel" because it was very proficient at hunting woodcock.

During this period, when only size separated the various classifications, it was possible to get a cocker, a field, and a springer spaniel all from the same litter. However, as dog shows came into being, the characteristics of each spaniel strain became more refined. Thus the individual spaniel breeds became more and more distinct from the whole spaniel family. Nevertheless, up until the 1870s, the only qualification for a dog to compete as a cocker was that it weigh less than 25 pounds (11.3 kg). Breeders quickly realized, however, that one further subdivision had to be made.

Cockers were originally designated as the group of smallest spaniels, but this classification also included the very small, or toy, spaniel. Since true cockers and toy spaniels were bred for entirely different purposes, these two groups were separated. The toys eventually became English toy spaniels, which were bred as companion animals, while the cockers maintained their status as sporting dogs.

Finally, in 1892, the cocker spaniel was recognized as a separate and distinct breed by the Kennel Club of England. There was still, however, one more change to come.

Cocker Spaniels in North America

In 1879 the most famous of all cockers was born. His name was Obo, and he was the offspring of a Sussex spaniel sire (father) and a field spaniel dam (mother). Obo was bred to a female cocker, which was taken to Canada while she was in whelp. Their son, Obo II, was then sold to a breeder in New Hampshire. Obo II was a black dog with a curly coat, especially on the shoulders and hindquarters, which also had profuse feathering. Obo II weighed 23½ pounds (10.7 kg), and he measured 9½ inches (24 cm) from foot to withers (see page 8). This dog proved to be the grandfather of all modern cockers. He was a direct ancestor of a cocker named Robinhurst Foreglow, and all winning cocker spaniels past and present are direct descendants of Foreglow and his four sons: Red Brucie, Champion Sandspring Surmise, Champion Midcliff Miracle Man, and the Canadian Champion Limestone Laddie. All other cocker

What Is a Cocker Spaniel?

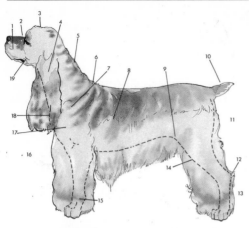

Exterior anatomy of the cocker spaniel

1. muzzle	6. withers	11. hindquarters	16. forequarters
2. stop	7. shoulder	12. hock	17. brisket
3. skull	8. rib cage	13. rear pastern	18. chest
4. ear	9. loin	14. stifle	19. cheek
5. neckline	10. docked tail	15. front pastern	

lines have completely disappeared from the breed over the years.

The Problem of Interbreeding

To satisfy the needs of a growing number of breeders on this continent, the American Spaniel Club was formed in 1881. Nevertheless, until 1935, there was still a certain amount of interbreeding between the cocker spaniels in England and those in the United States and Canada. Adding to the confusion, distinct differences began to arise between cockers bred strictly from English stock and those bred only from American stock.

In 1935 the English Cocker Spaniel Club of America (ECSA) was formed, not so much to promote the breed as to discourage the wanton interbreeding of the two varieties and to prevent their being shown against each other. Up until this time, the English cocker had been recognized as a variety of cocker but not as a different breed. One can imagine the confusion that must have occurred

when the same set of criteria was used to judge two different types of cocker spaniels. This situation was clearly not in the best interest of either type of cocker or its breeders.

Recognition of Two Breeds

Through extensive research into the pedigrees of English cocker spaniels the ECSA was able to ensure that the registered dogs had no mixture of American bloodlines. This research was completed in 1941, and five years later the American Kennel Club (AKC) recognized the English cocker spaniel as a separate breed. Likewise, the American cocker spaniel, or what is now called simply the cocker spaniel, was then properly identified, since the two varieties had previously been regarded as one.

Since 1946, the American Spaniel Club has had the responsibility of maintaining the integrity of the modern cocker spaniel, and has helped many cocker breeders through its establishment of the breed standard. The standard is a written description of cocker spaniels by which they are judged at dog shows. Cockers have competed in field trials in the United States since 1924, when the Cocker Spaniel Field Trial Club was formed.

Characteristics of the Breed

The following is an interpretation of the AKC-approved Standard for the cocker spaniel, which describes in writing the physical characteristics and temperament of the perfect cocker. It provides all the criteria by which the appearance and be-

There are few experiences that compare to owning a cocker puppy. Whether posing in a basket (top), chewing on their favorite toy (bottom left), or romping with Mom (bottom right), these adorable and active four to five-week-old-puppies are a joy to behold.

havior of the dog can be measured objectively. While reading this section, you should refer to the pictures and diagrams in this book. These illustrations will make it easier for you to learn about the cocker's anatomy.

It should be noted that each nation has its own set of breed standards. Thus, there are slight differences between the AKC's and the Kennel Club of England's standards for cockers. If you are showing your dog outside the United States, be sure that it conforms to the official standard of the host country.

General Appearance: As the smallest member of the sporting dog group, the cocker should be of ideal size and well balanced, with a compact and sturdy body. The cocker's head must be "cleanly chiseled and refined." When standing still, the cocker holds its head and forequarters high on muscular shoulders, while keeping its forelegs straight and perpendicular to the ground. Its back will slope down slightly toward the strong and muscular hindquarters.

Despite its small size the cocker is capable of considerable speed and has great endurance. Most importantly, however, the standard emphasizes that the dog must be "free and merry, sound, well balanced throughout, and in action show a keen inclination to work." The cocker's temperament should be calm and steady with no hint of shyness or fear. All these qualities should be reflected in the dog's general appearance.

Head and Facial Features: The head must be well proportioned and in balance with the rest of the body. To fulfill this image of balance, the distance from the tip of the nose to the stop (the sloped area between the forehead and the muzzle) is half

A cocker makes a wonderful companion for any youngster, for this breed is at its best when it has a child to play with and love. Likewise, the child will benefit by learning the responsibilities of pet ownership.

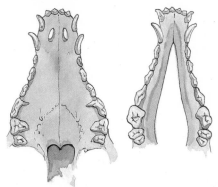

The upper (left) and lower (right) jaws of the cocker spaniel have 20 and 22 teeth, respectively. Missing or crooked teeth can be judged as faults in the show ring.

the distance from the stop, up and over the head, to the base of the skull. The cocker possesses a well-rounded skull with a tendency toward flatness. The stop should be steeply sloped, well pronounced, and positioned between well defined eyebrows. The bony structure below the eyes is clear-cut yet blends smoothly into the dog's cheeks.

The muzzle must appear square and be proportionately wide and long, with the upper and lower jaw of equal length. The upper lips are pendulous and hang down enough to cover the lower jaw. The teeth must be strong, sound, and meet in a "scissors bite."

The cocker's nose must be of a size proportional to the muzzle and face. It must be black in color for black and for black and tan cockers. Liver and white dogs may have brown noses, but the darker the better. The nose color should match the color of the eye rim. Because the cocker is a sporting dog that relies on its nose, the nostrils should be well defined.

The eyes, which are an important physical feature of the cocker spaniel, should convey an "intelligent, alert, soft, and appealing" expression. This expression is attained through proper eye color, size, and position. The eyes should be large and positioned to look straight ahead. The eyeballs must be round and full and set behind almond-shaped rims. The iris should be dark brown in color.

The size and shape of the cocker's ears are very important because they add to the overall character of this breed. They should begin no higher than a point even with the lower part of the eye. They should be "wide, long, and oval in shape," "of fine leather," and "well feathered." When the ears are pulled forward, the ends should reach the tip of the dog's nose.

Neck and Shoulders: The neck must be long enough to allow the dog to easily sniff the ground, an important feature for any hunting dog. It should also be well muscled, and the throat should be straight and void of loose-hanging skin. The neck should taper slightly as it moves from shoulders to head and should also arch slightly.

The shoulders should be set well back, at an angle perpendicular to the upper arm. This angle allows for free movement of the forelegs and a long stride. The shoulders should be sloping, well defined, and smooth and free of protruding joints.

The angle of the upper points of the shoulders (the withers) should allow "a wide spring of rib."

Overall Body Appearance: The cocker's body is small, compact, and sturdy and gives the impression of strength. The distance from the withers to the ground is about two inches more than the body length from the withers to the base of the tail. The back is strong and evenly sloped down toward the tail. The hips are wide, and the haunches are well rounded and muscular. The chest is deep, and the "well-sprung ribs" must come to a position lower than the dog's elbows. The rib cage must be large enough to house the heart and lungs adequately, yet it must not interfere with the movement of the forelegs.

The cocker possesses a docked (cut) tail, which is carried in a line continuous with the slope line of the back (or slightly higher). When the dog is at work, its tail should wag incessantly, reflecting its merry as well as industrious temperament.

The forelegs must be strongly boned, muscular, and held parallel to each other and straight. The

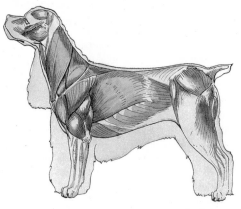

Although this fact is not always evident at first glance, the cocker spaniel is a sturdy, muscular hunting dog. This illustration shows the breed's extensive muscle structure, which is concealed by its lush and beautiful coat.

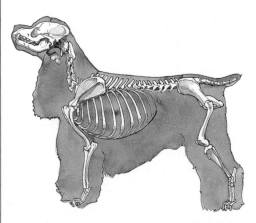

The skeletal structure of the cocker spaniel. If you refer to this illustration while reviewing the AKC Standard, you can better understand the cocker's anatomy and the way in which it allows for this breed's fluid movements.

What Is a Cocker Spaniel?

side view should show the elbows directly below the withers. The pasterns (the equivalent of human forearms) are short and strong. The hind legs are also well boned and muscular. The stifle (the equivalent of a knee) should have "good angulation," and the cocker must possess strong, powerful thighs. The stifle joint should be solid and should not allow for any "slippage" when the dog is in motion or is standing still. The hocks (the points where the lower legs join with the feet) are strong and low set, and are parallel when viewed from behind. The feet, large, round, and firm with "horny pads," should turn neither in nor out. All dew claws can be removed.

Coat: The cocker's body coat is of medium length and is dense enough to provide protection from the elements, while its head hairs are short and fine. Ample feathering should appear on the dog's ears, legs, abdomen, and chest but should not hide the cocker's true features or movement. (This point is often given much leeway by the judges; it is discussed in more detail on page 32.)

The standard also states that the texture of the dog's coat is extremely important. "The coat is silky, flat or slightly wavy, and of a texture which permits easy care." The coat should not be too wavy or curly or "cottony" textured.

Color and Markings: Cocker spaniels vary greatly in color, and thus each variety has its own acceptable standards.

The *black variety* is jet black with little or no shadings of brown or liver. Small amounts of white on chest or throat are penalized. All other white markings disqualify the dog from bench competitions.

Any solid color other than black must be a uniform shade, with lighter colored feathering acceptable. White markings are dealt with in the same way as for the black variety.

Black and tans have definite tan markings on jet black bodies. The markings must be distinct and plainly visible, and can range in color from light cream to darkest red. The markings are restricted

in amount to ten percent or less of the body area; more extensive markings result in disqualification. Tan markings that are not easily visible, or a lack of markings in any of the following locations, will disqualify the dog:

1. Over the eye
2. On the sides of the muzzle and on the cheeks
3. On the undersides of the ears
4. On all feet and legs
5. Under the tail

The presence or absence of marking on the chest is not penalized. Tan on the muzzle that extends upward over the snout will be penalized. White markings will result in penalties or disqualifications as in the solid varieties.

Particolored varieties have "two or more definite colors appearing in clearly defined markings, distinctly distributed over the body." Disqualification will result if the primary color covers 90 percent of the dog. Secondary colors that are limited to a single location on the body also disqualify the dog. The particolor variety includes the cockers that are commonly refered to as roans or tricolors.

Movement: The following is taken directly from the AKC Standard, which I consider the best description possible:

"The Cocker Spaniel, though the smallest of the sporting dogs, possesses a typical sporting dog gait. Prerequisite to good movement is balance between the front and rear assemblies. He drives with his strong, powerful rear quarters and is properly constructed in the shoulders and forelegs so that he can reach forward without constriction in a full stride to counterbalance the driving force from the rear. Above all, his gait is coordinated, smooth, and effortless. The dog must cover ground with his action and excessive animation should never be mistaken for proper gait."

Height: The ideal height at the withers is 15 inches (38 cm) for a male and 14 inches (35.6 cm) for a female cocker. Height variation can be no greater than ½ inch (1.4 cm) above and below the ideal. A cocker of excessive height will be disqualified; insufficient height incurs a penalty.

Differences Between the American and the English Cocker Spaniel

Although the differences between the American and the English cocker are quite obvious to the show judge, they are not always clear to the novice. The English cocker is slightly larger, the maximum height of both males and females being ½ to 1½ inches (1.4–3.8 cm) greater than that of their American counterparts.

The most obvious difference, however, can be seen in the head shapes. Compared to the English dog, the American cocker has a distinctly domed skull, as well as a deep pronounced stop and more clearly defined eyebrows. Also, the American dog's lips tend to hang down farther and more loosely, and its eyes are slightly larger and set more to look straight ahead than those of the English cocker spaniel. Finally, the American cocker carries a much more profuse coat than its English cousin.

Is the Cocker Spaniel the Dog for Me?

Making an Intelligent Choice

Attributes and Needs of the Cocker Spaniel

The cocker spaniel's history as a "gundog" has had a great influence on its temperament and personality. Generations of companionship between hunter and cocker have ingrained in the breed many traits that reflect this close relationship. Like most hunting dogs, cockers are highly intelligent and therefore relatively easy to train. They are a bright, sturdy, and loyal breed with an assertive yet stable personality. They also possess an innate sensitivity to the moods of their masters. These traits make the cocker an ideal dog for the first-time owner. In addition, the cocker spaniel's ability to adapt readily to the role of family companion makes it a wonderful addition to a family with small children. These qualities, combined with the pure beauty of the breed and the wide variety of colors available, provide some explanation of why the cocker spaniel has become one of the most popular dogs of our time.

While owning a dog may seem completely natural, it must be pointed out that not every breed of dog is right for every type of human life-style. In fact, there are certain life-styles that are not suitable for any breed of dog. It is vital to both the physical and mental health of a dog that the animal be given a suitable home and the attention it needs to form a proper bond with its master.

For all its fine attributes, the cocker may not be the ideal pet for everyone. The cocker spaniel is a long haired breed and requires frequent grooming to keep its coat in top condition. The same thick coat that is designed to protect the dog from the elements is also, unfortunately, designed to collect dirt and mud. Another disadvantage to owning a long haired dog is that, when it sheds, it leaves long hairs all over the carpet and furniture. This is something to keep in mind, especially if you or anyone else in your family suffers from allergies.

Being a hunting breed, the cocker spaniel needs to be kept in peak physical condition. Beneath its soft, dense coat lies a rugged, muscular, and powerful body. To maintain its muscle tone and mental sharpness, the cocker needs adequate exercise. While this breed is small enough to adapt to virtually any housing arrangement, you will need to have a place where you can bring your dog for its regular workout.

In saying this, I do not mean to imply that the cocker cannot adapt to life in a city apartment, with its exercise limited to short walks at the end of a leash. In fact, the cocker will easily adapt to any life-style that keeps it close to its master. However, this breed is at its best when it is tramping through the woods or romping through the park, following its keen sense of smell as it bounds from one adventure to another. The cocker spaniel requires a constant challenge to keep it mentally sharp; when it is kept in this condition, there are few breeds that can compare.

All of the traits mentioned in this section are latent in every cocker. It is up to the owner, however, to bring them to the surface so that they become a dominant part of the dog's personality. Bringing out the best your cocker has to offer will take time, energy, patience, and understanding.

Factors to Consider Before Purchasing a Dog

Whether or not to buy a dog is an important decision. Many people are not aware, at the time of purchase, of the responsibilities of dog ownership. To buy a dog impulsively is an irresponsible act and often leads to an unhappy relationship for both the dog and its owner. Therefore, I urge you to carefully consider the following points before you decide to get a cocker spaniel.

First, keep in mind that owning a dog is a long-term commitment. A cocker may live for a dozen years; and with recent advances in animal nutrition

Is the Cocker Spaniel the Dog for Me?

and health care, the average lifespan of the breed will only increase.

Second, be aware that a great deal of time, energy, and patience is required to raise, train, and properly care for a cocker spaniel. While this breed is renowned for its ability to learn, training requires a strict regimen in order to optimize your dog's performance. In addition, your dog will require daily walks and grooming.

Should you decide to purchase a cocker puppy, you must be willing to rearrange your daily schedule to meet the dog's needs. Puppies must be watched much more carefully than adult dogs, and they require several small feedings each day.

Third, whether you are looking for a puppy or an adult dog, you will have to make plans for housing your pet both indoors and out. If you do not have a large yard, you will need access to a park or woods where you can take your dog for exercise. If you have a suitable yard, you may have to build a fence or a run to prevent your dog from straying.

Fourth, owning a cocker brings additional expenses. Besides the initial price of the dog (see page 20), there is the cost of equipment such as bowls, leashes, collars, and brushes. Food may cost as much as $30 per month. There will be license and registration fees, veterinarian's bills, and incidental expenses such as the cost of building a fence or run in your yard.

As you can see, purchasing a dog should never be a "spur of the moment" decision. Rather, to buy or not to buy must be thought through in a careful and sensible fashion.

If you have any additional questions about owning a cocker, you should contact a local chapter of the American Spaniel Club (ASC). This organization can supply you with detailed answers to all your inquiries, as well as with a list of reputable breeders in your area whom you can visit before you make your decision.

But then, when you have decided that you want to own a dog and that the cocker spaniel is the right breed for you—wouldn't you know it, there are more choices to be made!

It is the responsibility of all dog owners to clean up after their pets, and in some towns the law requires them to do so.

A Puppy or an Adult?

Speaking as someone who has endured the experience, I honestly believe that there is no greater satisfaction in dog ownership (except maybe winning your first dog show) than acquiring a tiny, fragile, adorable, eight-week-old ball of fur and energy, and raising it to be an obedient, loyal, and loving companion. Notice, however, that I used the term "endured."

Let it be known at the outset that raising puppies is not always a bowl of cherries, especially for the novice. Housebreaking alone can become, quite literally, a nightmare if it is not done correctly. (This book describes ways to make your nights with a puppy a lot quieter. See page 30.) There may be additional problems as well, not the least of which is the teething puppy. Personally, I feel that, when you weigh the pros and cons of raising a

Is the Cocker Spaniel the Dog for Me?

puppy, the pros win by a landslide, but in truth the experience is not for everyone.

Cocker spaniel puppies are playful, intelligent, and adventurous little creatures, and with the proper training techniques you can use these qualities to your advantage. By making training sessions resemble a game, you can teach a cocker puppy an incredible number of commands or tricks—and your dog will love you all the more for the lessons.

There are other advantages to raising a dog from puppyhood. If you have children, raising a puppy is a great way to bring the family together and to teach the kids the responsibilities of pet ownership. Moreover, starting with a puppy will allow you to "mold" the dog to suit your personal or family life-style.

Another benefit to raising a puppy is the satisfaction you will get from a job well done. You will experience this satisfaction each and every time your cocker fetches its stick and releases it into your hand, or when the dog comes eagerly when you call its name or stops on a dime when you tell it to halt. Truly, the best way to obtain a well-trained pet is to train it yourself.

While raising a puppy properly may sound simple, do not kid yourself. To bring out the best a puppy has to offer takes time, patience, energy, and dedication. If you work diligently with a cocker puppy, you will eventually be rewarded with a loyal and loving companion. However, if you are lax in your training, you will probably end up with an unruly dog—a situation that is not very good for either owner or animal.

With these facts in mind, one can easily see the advantages of getting an adult dog. A well-trained adult cocker spaniel makes a wonderful pet, especially for those who do not have the time or the desire to train a puppy. A housebroken adult makes a marvelous companion for the elderly, for it requires little supervision. Also, a well-adjusted adult cocker will have little trouble acclimating itself to a new owner and environment. As long as

these dogs get the love and attention they need, they will usually make the change without a hitch.

The greatest drawback to owning an older cocker is that you may find it difficult to break the dog of any bad habits it has already acquired. While this book contains some tips on teaching an old dog new tricks, be warned in advance that the lessons are not easy.

Selecting a Show Dog

If, in obtaining a dog, you have the express intent of showing it in the ring, there are basically two options. The first is to select a puppy based on its parents' pedigree and to raise it yourself. In this case you will have the advantage of self-satisfaction at your achievement, and you will also encounter less expense. However, there is always the chance that a late-arising fault in the puppy may ruin your ring hopes. The other option is to purchase a mature show dog, for which you will be expected to pay significantly more. This second option, of course, assures you of getting the quality and beauty of a ring dog.

A Male or a Female?

If you are getting a cocker strictly as a companion animal, there are a few differences between the sexes you may wish to consider. Female cockers tend to be slightly smaller, slightly more sedate, and at times a little more affectionate and sensitive than their male counterparts, which are sometimes a bit more independent. However, these differences may not even be noticeable unless you own both a male and a female at the same time.

The choice of sex is much more important should you plan on becoming a breeder. If you are considering starting a kennel, then, of course, you

17

Is the Cocker Spaniel the Dog for Me?

will want to get a female, so that you can breed her to obtain your stock.

If, however, you decide to get a female cocker spaniel but do not plan to breed her, you should have her spayed for several reasons. Spaying will reduce the risk that your female dog will suffer from such ailments as breast tumors, ovarian cysts, and false pregnancies. By spaying her you will also avoid the messiness that may occur when she is in season. It is important to note that, if you plan to enter your female in dog shows, she will be disqualified if she is spayed; however, a spayed dog may compete in field and obedience trials.

Regardless of sex, if you are getting a cocker spaniel strictly to be a companion animal (to be neither shown nor bred), you should have it neutered. There are an alarming number of homeless dogs in the United States because of the irresponsibility of many dog owners. It is important that all pet owners take steps to prevent the proliferation of unwanted animals.

How to Buy a Cocker Spaniel

If you wish to buy a high-quality cocker spaniel, it is of the utmost importance that you deal with a well-established and reputable source. A quality dog comes from good breeding stock, has been well cared for, and is healthy and free of the genetic ailments that plague some breeds. You can get a list of reliable cocker spaniel breeders in your area from the American Kennel Club (AKC) or from the secretary of the American Spaniel Club (ASC). Be aware, however, that while it is more convenient to obtain a cocker from a local breeder or reputable pet store (which may deal directly with top breeders), traveling the extra distance to visit as many breeders or pet shops as possible sometimes pays dividends.

Start by making appointments with all of the breeders or stores on your list. The objective, while visiting each facility, is to inspect both the dogs and their housing. Reliable breeders and store managers are very proud of their stock, so do not be afraid to ask questions. These people understand that the quality of their cockers is a direct reflection of their concern for their dogs and the care they give them, and a conscientious breeder or pet shop manager will make every effort to answer your inquiries. Not only are they concerned about satisfying a customer, but also they want to make sure that their dogs find safe homes and caring masters.

Like many other breeds, cocker spaniels are subject to certain hereditary ailments that arise from time to time. A reputable breeder, however, will never breed any dog known to carry one of these defects. Ask the breeders or pet shop managers you visit if their dogs have been checked and cleared of genetically linked eye diseases. All dogs over two years old should also have been examined to ensure that they do not suffer from hip dysplasia. While this problem is more often associated with larger breeds, it has been known to afflict a small number of cockers. Finally, be sure the dogs have been tested for Von Willebrand's disease, which affects blood-clotting ability. (A more detailed discussion of all of these hereditary ailments is given in the chapter entitled "Ailments and Illnesses.")

While visiting each breeder or pet shop, check the conditions under which the cocker spaniels are kept. Make sure that the facilities are spacious and clean. If you are visiting a breeder, look at the adult cockers to make sure that all of the breeding stock is happy and healthy. These dogs should be clean and have thick, shiny coats, and should exhibit the sturdiness, balance, and happy, attentive temperament that typifies this breed.

Only after you have questioned the breeder and inspected the kennels and the adult dogs should you look at the puppies. Many a potential cocker owner has made the mistake of going into a breeder's kennel and running straight off to see the puppies. Be warned that it is extremely hard to form an objective opinion as to the quality of the breeder when you are enthralled by the antics of

Is the Cocker Spaniel the Dog for Me?

these dark-eyed, floppy-eared fluff balls. Stay cool! Try to remember that, while all cocker puppies are adorable, there is more to this breed than just outward appearances.

Avoid buying a puppy impulsively. Be sure to check out each and every breeder or pet shop on your list. Remember that the time you spend finding a physically healthy and well-adjusted puppy will save you a lot of anguish later on. By the same token, never be tempted to buy a cocker spaniel on the basis of price. There are usually very good reasons why some dogs are less expensive. A lower price usually indicates that the dog was bred strictly for profit by an inexperienced breeder, or that it is in poor health. The extra money you spend for a high-quality dog at the time of purchase is often less than the additional veterinary bills that a low-priced puppy will incur.

Once you have confidence in the quality of the breeder or pet shop, it is time to consider which one of the puppies you will take home to its new family.

Selecting the Right Puppy for You

As you are aware, cockers come in a wide variety of color patterns, including solid colors (black, red, cream, buff, and liver) as well as particolors (black and white, black and tan, and a few liver and whites) and even a tricolor (black, white, and tan). Although color may influence your choice of a puppy, it should never be your primary concern. There are more important factors you need to consider.

First, make sure that all of the puppies in the litter are healthy. Their coats should be smooth and shiny. Now check the puppy you have in mind to buy. Examine its eyes and ears, making sure that they are not running or have any signs of discharge. The eyes should be bright and have a friendly expression. Examine the nose to make sure it is not running. The nose of a healthy cocker puppy is usually wet, but a dry nose does not always indicate

illness. Check the teeth and gums for unusual bleeding. Then look critically at the puppy's physical build. While cocker puppies are small, they should still appear to be sturdy, rugged little creatures.

Finally, observe the puppy's temperament. A cocker spaniel puppy should be friendly, alert, eager, and curious. Its tail should be wagging, and there should be no sign of either aggression or extreme shyness. Cockers are hunting dogs and as such should never be unfriendly toward, or afraid of, unthreatening people.

Another good indicator of the puppy's temperament is the behavior of its mother. After all, much of the puppy's physical and behavioral traits are inherited from its parents. Watch how the mother reacts with the breeder. She should exhibit all of the behavioral traits that characterize this hunting breed. The mother should appear eager to please her master and show no signs of fear of people.

If the puppy appears to be in good health and of sound temperament, you should next check the pedigree. This written record of the dog's recent ancestry has special notations marking all show champions that are part of the dog's family tree. While a pedigree with many champions is impressive, the status of the dogs that precede your puppy by two or three generations should receive most of your attention.

If the pedigree appears satisfactory, the next step is to ask the breeder for a written record of when the puppy was wormed and vaccinated. This information is important for later use by your veterinarian.

Throughout the transaction of purchasing your puppy, you should attempt to build a good rapport with the breeder. Should you need any advice down the road, the person who bred and raised your dog can be a reliable source of help.

A final note on selecting a puppy: It is always a good idea to choose a puppy with a temperament that will suit your life-style. As I have already mentioned, all cocker puppies are cute and cuddly.

Is the Cocker Spaniel the Dog for Me?

However, if you watch the litter very carfully, you will begin to see subtle differences from one puppy to the next. While watching the puppies play together, you will notice which ones are bolder and which are more submissive. If you have an active family life-style or have children, you may want to choose a livelier or bolder puppy that will not be intimidated by a hubbub of human activity. If you lead a quiet life, then perhaps a calmer and more sedate puppy is for you.

How Much Will the Dog Cost?

While the initial purchase price of a cocker spaniel will vary, you should expect to spend at least $250. Show-quality puppies from champion-caliber lineage may sell for as much as $1000. In general, the better the bloodlines, the higher the cost. Likewise, the older a puppy, the more expensive it will be because the breeder has invested more time and money in it.

People often wonder why well-raised purebred dogs are so expensive. The answer is quite simple. As you have already learned, the cocker spaniel, like other purebreds, has a special place in history and culture. It also has certain physical and mental characteristics that make the breed unique. Keeping and raising a purebred requires care that goes far beyond basic food and shelter. It is the breeder's objective to "create" the perfect dog, and this requires skill, time, patience, education, and, of course, a proven track record. If one considers only a reasonable hourly wage for the time breeders

spend on their dogs, it is evident that these "expensive" dogs are really sold at bargain prices. The warning bears repetition: Beware of "cheap" dogs. The old adage "You get what you pay for" is all too true when buying a dog.

As stated earlier, food for your cocker may cost as much as $30 a month, and there are also licensing fees, for which you should check with your local town hall or animal shelter. You will also need to purchase certain equipment for feeding, housing, and grooming your cocker.

Veterinarian costs must also be considered. A cocker will require annual immunizations and checkups to ensure its ongoing health. In addition, your pet may have to be wormed. If your puppy should become sick or be injured, additional, perhaps costly medical treatment may be neeeded.

Finally, you will have to pay a fee to register your dog with the American Kennel Club, and there are annual dues if you join the American Spaniel Club. Should you decide to either show or breed your dog, the process can become truly expensive. In summary, the costs involved in owning a cocker spaniel go far beyond the initial purchase price.

A final note on the cost of quality puppies: Keep in mind that you are spending a reasonable amount to ensure that your cocker is healthy and sound and is a proud representative of its breed. But, in truth, the dog does not know how much money you paid for it, nor does it care. If you start with a quality puppy, and give it the care, attention, and affection it needs, it will freely give back to you all of its love and loyalty. What a priceless dividend on your investment!

Housing and Supplies

Requirements of a House Dog

Like their wild relatives, dogs are very territorial and, as such, require a living space, or "denning" area, that they can call their own. Luckily, because of its size, the cocker does not require as large an area as do bigger breeds. Your dog's indoor territory will consist of its feeding and sleeping areas, which offer your beloved pet a refuge where it can eat in peace and rest whenever the need arises. The key to selecting the proper location for these areas is to find a place that will afford your dog a comfortable, secure feeling, yet accords well with the life-style of the two-legged inhabitants of your home.

To help your cocker feel secure, you should place its bed in a room that is not subject to heavy human traffic, but in which the dog will not be isolated from contact with people. It is also advisable to choose a room where the dog can easily be confined when you go to bed or leave the house. In locating the bed, a corner of the room is preferred because the dog is then protected on two sides, adding to its sense of security. You should avoid placing the bed in direct sunlight or in a drafty location.

Your cocker's feeding area should also provide a sense of security, and therefore you can follow the same rules used to select a sleeping area. It is recommended, however, that you feed your dog in a room that can be easily cleaned, such as the kitchen. It is vitally important that your cocker be left in peace in its eating area. Nervous dogs have trouble digesting food properly, and this difficulty will eventually lead to other biological problems, which can be quite messy.

Take time and use thought in selecting your cocker's eating and sleeping areas so that they will not have to be changed later on. Your dog will not feel comfortable or secure if it must constantly search for a quiet place to sleep or eat. Permanent and peaceful sleeping and eating areas will help prevent undue stress on your cocker and allow you to avoid the physical and behavioral problems associated with a tense, unhappy animal.

Once you have decided where your dog will sleep, you must choose a type of bed. The choice between a sleeping box and a cage is often determined by your method of housebreaking. (See the chapter entitled "Basic and Advanced Training.") Personally, I am a staunch advocate of using a cage. Not only does a cage make housebreaking easier, but also it is invaluable for transporting or disciplining your puppy.

Dogs are instinctively "denning" animals and, as such, feel much more secure in the confined, well-protected space of a cage than in an open sleeping box. The cage will become your cocker's "home," and you will find that your dog will seek it out voluntarily whenever the animal feels the need to rest. Your cocker's cage should be approximately 20 inches (50 cm) high by 24 inches (61 cm) wide by 30 inches (76 cm) long. The bars should be welded close enough together to prevent a puppy's head from squeezing through and getting caught.

If you decide not to use a cage, purchase a sleeping box or a sleeping basket (the latter may offer your dog some added security) big enough to accommodate a spread-out adult cocker. If you build your own sleeping box, use only nonsplintering hardwoods and make sure that the box allows

Cocker spaniels take easily to cages, which offer the dog a safe and protected place to sleep.

easy access to your puppy or adult cocker. Because many paints and stains can be toxic, leave the box unfinished.

If you have a puppy, you should line the bottom of its sleeping quarters with plastic or an old piece of linoleum, covered with a good layer of cedar shavings or shredded newspapers topped with an old blanket. This will provide your dog with a very comfortable bed that can be easily cleaned or disposed of in case of "accidents."

Outdoor Needs

Being originally bred for hunting, the cocker spaniel has little trouble adapting to life outdoors. Its coat is perfectly designed to protect it from the elements, keep it warm in the colder weather, and prevent it from overheating in the summer. Cockers are at their best when they are outdoors and have some room to roam, and many cocker owners appreciate the fact that they can keep their dogs outside when they are away from home.

If you decide to keep your dog outside while you are away, you must be sure that it cannot escape your property. If your yard is not adequately fenced, you must provide your cocker with a run.

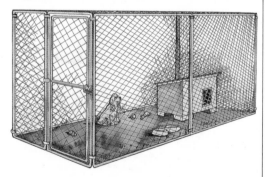

This run, complete with shelter, can provide a cocker with a place to exercise as well as protection from the elements.

The run should be at least 4 feet (1.3 m) wide by 12 feet (4 m) long by 6 feet (2 m) high and enclosed by a chain link fence. While the height of the fence may seem excessive for a cocker, remember that the fence also serves to keep other animals away from your pet. You can bury boards around the base of the run to prevent digging under the fence.

The bottom of the run should be covered with a few inches of smooth stone to provide drainage and to prevent the ground from becoming muddy. Avoid using a concrete base, which will retain the smell of urine. It is also very important that a portion of the run provides your dog with shade and protection from the elements.

A properly constructed doghouse is the best form of outdoor shelter. The floor should be raised several inches above the ground in order to keep the house dry and prevent invasion from insects. The dimensions must be large enough to comfortably accommodate a stretched-out adult dog, yet not so large that during cold weather the space cannot be heated with warmth from the dog's body. A cocker

This doghouse is cleverly designed with a hinged lid for easy cleaning, and a layout that offers added protection from the rain and wind.

Housing and Supplies

spaniel requires a shelter that has the same dimensions as its cage (see the preceding section).

Whether you choose to buy a doghouse or to build it yourself, there are additional features that you may want to consider. A hinged roof will give you better access and make cleaning much easier. The opening should be covered with a flap of canvas or a blanket to keep out the wind and rain; and if you live in a cold climate, the doghouse should be fully insulated. When positioning the structure, have the opening face south, out of the cold north winds.

To facilitate cleaning the shelter, I recommend lining the floor with a piece of linoleum or another easy-to-clean material. Then add a layer of cedar shavings, and cover it with an old blanket.

Regardless of how well insulated or weatherproof your doghouse is, I do not recommend keeping your pet outdoors during cold weather for a long period of time. While cockers are hardy creatures, they can catch colds and become sick if subjected to nasty weather. For this reason it is wise to have an indoor space put aside for the dog on foul-weather days.

Additional Equipment and Accessories

If dogs could talk, I am sure that they would say that the most important items of equipment you should get for them are food and water dishes, preferably ones that are sturdy and nonbreakable. Bowls are available in stainless steel, plastic, and ceramics. If choosing a ceramic bowl, you must be absolutely sure that it was not fired with a lead-based glaze. Also, unless you enjoy cleaning your floors three times a day, make sure that your dog's dishes are not tippable.

A collar and a leash are also mandatory equipment. Collars and leashes come in a variety of sizes and are made of several different materials, including leather, nylon, and metal chain. The cocker owner need not worry about the dog's strength and therefore needs only a well-made leather or nylon collar and leash. Leather and nylon equipment, however, should be checked from time to time because it tends to deteriorate with age. If you are getting a puppy, you may also find it necessary to buy collars of different sizes to accommodate the dog's growing body. You may also consider buying a special collar equipped with a slip ring, which will help during training sessions.

You may also wish to have several leashes on hand. For regular walks or training, you need a leash that is only several feet long. For outdoor fun, a long leash equipped with an automatic reel permits more freedom. If you have a puppy, you should check its leash regularly for chew marks; chewing can quickly weaken a nylon or leather leash. Also, be sure that your puppy never chews on the leash's metal clips, which can damage its teeth.

I recommend using reflective tape or tags on both the collar and the walking leashes. These will render both you and your dog more visible to car drivers and thereby make your nighttime walks much safer. You should attach to your dog's collar an identity tag that gives your name, address, and telephone number. This inexpensive tag could prove invaluable should your beloved pet ever become lost.

Only very rarely will a cocker spaniel require a muzzle. However, it may be useful to have on hand should your pet or another neighborhood dog ever become injured. A dog in severe pain may act unpredictably and may snap at its owner, so it is best to be prepared. You may also find a muzzle necessary if you travel with your pet to foreign countries; in some places it is required by law that all dogs wear muzzles in public. When buying a muzzle, select one that can be adjusted to fit both young and adult cockers.

Additional equipment and accessories that you should have on hand are flea spray and tweezers to combat external parasites, and grooming supplies. All of these items are listed in detail in the sections on external parasites (pages 47–48) and on grooming (pages 30–34).

To avoid added stress to what is already likely to be a hectic day, you should buy all your cocker's equipment before you bring your new dog home. Then pick out a single place to store the items so that they will be easily accessible when the need for any of them arises.

Toys

As a new dog owner, you should never underestimate the importance of toys for your pet. Toys play a vital role in keeping your dog both physically and mentally fit. They can give your cocker added exercise, and many have the ability to keep your pet busy and entertained for long periods of time—an added benefit on occasions when you cannot closely supervise your cocker. For instance, when you are cooking dinner, you can keep your dog out of mischief simply by giving it a favorite toy to play with.

While it may seem strange, toys also have some psychological benefits for your cocker. In the wild, doglike creatures are organized in a social structure where the dominant animals become pack leaders while smaller, weaker animals are followers. During training sessions you will actually be enforcing your superiority as master over your pet. Eventually your cocker will come to understand that all of the members of your family are above it in the social structure of your household. In this situation, toys can serve as objects for your dog to dominate, enabling it to work out the frustration that it may feel from always having to be submissive to the humans in your household.

Toys serve an additional purpose for a cocker puppy in that they help sharpen its hunting and survival skills. Even though your cocker may not have received any formal training as a hunting dog, you will notice that the breed has inherited instinctive behavior patterns common to most gundogs. Your puppy will naturally stalk, attempt to flush, and finally capture its toys just as an older bird dog may do with living prey.

If you are still unconvinced of the importance of toys to your pet's health, here is one last reason to get them: simply put, a rawhide bone is much cheaper than new furniture. Puppies, especially those that are teething, are apt to spend a lot of their spare time chewing in an attempt to strengthen their teeth and jaw muscles. Rawhide bones, as well as many other dog toys, are excellent objects on which your dog can satisfy its urge to chew, thereby avoiding teeth marks in your Chippendale.

Since a puppy's teeth are sharp, you will have to keep a watchful eye on its toys. Rawhide bones must be replaced before they become small enough to swallow whole. Avoid soft toys that can be shredded and swallowed by an active puppy. Swallowing large or foreign objects can cause choking or a blockage in the puppy's digestive system.

Be sure that all of your cocker's "chew" toys are designed for dogs and are made of nontoxic materials. Remember that many forms of plastic are toxic, and soft woods tend to splinter. To be safe, avoid all painted or varnished toys, as these may contain chemicals that can be harmful to your pet.

Other types of toys can be created from simple household objects. Playing "hide-and-seek" using a cardboard box or paper shopping bag can keep your puppy busy for hours. Tennis balls also make good toys, because they are durable enough to stand up to a puppy's teeth, yet too big to be swallowed whole. Obviously, you should avoid letting your puppy have small or breakable objects. Also, it is inadvisable to give your puppy personal items that have your scent on them, such as old slippers or sneakers. While the cocker spaniel is an intelligent dog, chances are that your pet will not be able to tell the difference between your old and new footwear. Many a dog owner has come home from a hard day's work, only to find a chewed-up surprise in the middle of the bedroom floor.

Cockers are fun-loving dogs and, as such, cannot seem to get enough toys. Each additional toy becomes an entirely new adventure. In fact, cockers like new toys so much that they may even "accidentally" misplace the old ones. Moreover, cockers have an uncanny way of obtaining more toys from their sympathetic masters. After seeing the dog look sad and sulk around the house in a vain search for entertainment, even the most hardhearted cocker owner gives in and finds his or her pet a new plaything.

While I used to think that this behavior was an isolated phenomenon, cocker owners have convinced me that it is the rule rather than the exception. In fact, a friend of mine has a cocker that loves to demonstrate this behavior for visitors. The dog's owner starts by pulling his couch away from the wall and removing an assorted cache of hidden bones, balls, and squeaky toys, which he places in the middle of the floor. Within minutes, his black cocker, Angus, will enter the room and pick up a toy, play with it for a while, and then leave the room with the toy in his mouth. Each time Angus returns empty-mouthed. Once the cocker has cleared the room of every toy, he returns, stares at his master with large black, sad eyes, and begins to sulk. After a short time his owner gives him a new plaything, and then Angus becomes one of the liveliest and happiest dogs I have ever seen. Strangely enough, however, after a few weeks, this new toy also mysteriously disappears.

Caring for a Cocker Spaniel

Preparing for a Puppy

It is inevitable that your first days home with your new puppy will be rather hectic. To reduce the worry, confusion, and stress to both you and your pet, certain precautions should be taken.

First, if at all possible, visit your puppy several times before you bring it home to help it become familiar with your presence. Recognizing a friendly face will help reduce the stress the puppy will feel when it finds itself in a totally new environment away from its mother and siblings.

Second, lay in the supplies and prepare the housing for your pet. Find out from the breeder or pet shop manager what kind of food the puppy has been fed and buy a supply ahead of time. Using the same kind of food will reduce the chances of dietary upsets. At the same time you should also purchase all the equipment and accessories mentioned in the preceeding chapter and store them in a convenient place. Then lay out your puppy's eating and sleeping areas.

The third and fourth steps in preparing for the new arrival are to "puppy-proof" your home, and to make sure that your friends and family understand the basic rules of handling a cocker puppy.

Finally, if at all possible, bring the puppy home on a weekend or at another time when you have a few days off. This way you can stay close to the little newcomer and properly supervise it for a few days in a row.

The Rules of Puppy Safety

Before you bring your puppy home, review the following seven rules with your family and friends. In addition to preventing injury to the puppy, these rules will help your new pet to feel comfortable and safe in your home.

1. Avoid unnecessary excitement. New owners have a tendency to invite everyone they know over to see their puppy, and young visitors will usually run around, screaming with glee. Let the puppy adjust to its new surroundings before you subject it to numerous strangers.
2. Prohibit rough play. Puppies are very fragile creatures and should be handled with care until they grow larger and more mature. Therefore you should avoid overhandling, and make sure that children do not prod or poke the puppy, probe into its ears, or subject it to any other rough handling.
3. Be sure that everyone in your household knows the proper way to lift and carry the puppy. (The proper technique is explained in detail on page 35 in this chapter.) If any visitors express a desire to pick up the puppy, instruct them how to do so.
4. Avoid picking up the puppy too much. Allow it to do its own walking as much as possible, so that it will get needed exercise and added confidence in its own physical abilities.
5. Do not give bones or other very hard objects to a young puppy. Until the puppy reaches about six months of age, it has only its milk teeth and cannot chew hard objects such as meat bones.
6. Do not subject your puppy to unnecessary heights. Avoid placing it on tables, counters, or beds, since a fall could be disastrous. When it is necessary to place the puppy on an elevated surface, as when you are examining or grooming it, someone must be present the entire time to ensure the puppy's safety.
7. Try never to leave the puppy unsupervised during the first few weeks.

Cockers are naturals at retrieving and can be taught to "fetch" with relative ease. Although retrieving and relinquishing an object are requirements of the obedience trials, they are important lessons for all hunting dogs to learn.

Caring for a Cocker Spaniel

By following these rules, you can keep your puppy from harm and increase its confidence in its owner and family. The faster your dog feels comfortable and safe in its new home, the faster it will begin to act like the loving companion that you envision.

"Puppy-proofing" Your Home

An essential step in preparing for your new friend is to make sure you bring it into a "puppy-friendly" environment. When "puppy-proofing" your home, keep in mind that a young dog is an extremely inquisitive creature and will investigate every square inch of your house or apartment, using its nose to sniff, paws to touch, and teeth to chew just about everything it encounters. Therefore, you will have to remove all potential hazards from your puppy's reach—and you will be amazed at just how small a nook or how high a cranny your puppy can get into.

Remove all sharp objects such as staples, nails, and broken glass from your home. Be sure that all electrical cords and wires are out of your puppy's reach; the shock received from chewing on a live electric wire can severely injure and even kill a dog. You should also place all poisons such as paints, disinfectants, insecticides, cleaners, and antifreeze in a location that is completely secure from infiltration by a determined puppy.

Once you have puppy-proofed your house, check your yard and garage and again remove all potentially harmful materials. For your puppy's safety, be thorough when checking for hazardous

Scent discriminations and retrieving are lessons that are important to all hunting dogs and a requirement at field trials. Top: This cocker must find the barbell that has the proper scent and return it to its master. Bottom left: This dog is being taught to drop the object on recall. Bottom right: A cocker must relinquish its "prey" to its master on command.

situations, and follow this adage: "When in doubt (of an object's safety), move it out (of your puppy's reach)."

The First Days Home

The big day has finally arrived—you are to pick up your puppy and bring it to its new home. When you go to the breeder or pet dealer be sure to bring your cocker's collar, leash, and traveling cage with you. It is extremely unwise to let your puppy loose in your car on the journey home, no matter how short the distance. If you will have to travel for several hours, bring along a little food and water, and plan on making a stop or two to allow your puppy to eat, drink, and relieve itself.

If you have to travel for a considerable distance, there is always the chance that your puppy will become carsick. As a precaution, bring extra blankets to line your puppy's traveling cage in case of accidents. You will also need a short-bristled brush and some towels to clean the dog's coat. Do not wash the dog with water, because it can cause a chill.

Once you have reached home, put your puppy on the leash, let it walk around outside for a while, and take it to the site you have chosen for its elimination area. Do not rush the puppy inside; give it plenty of time to relieve itself. In this way there will be one less thing for you to worry about when the puppy is taken indoors.

Make your puppy's first days in your house calm ones. Keep visitors to a minimum, and allow your little friend time to get used to its new family before you introduce it to neighbors and friends. Since your puppy will already be somewhat frightened and apprehensive, having been taken away from the comfort of its mother and siblings, it should be protected from additional stress. A calm, quiet atmosphere will help to reassure your puppy that it will be safe and loved in its new home.

Let your pet spend its first few hours exploring your house or apartment. Take every opportunity to

29

speak soft words and pet it reassuringly. Show the puppy where its food and water dishes are; and if it wants to eat or drink, let it do so in peace. To reduce the effects of stress on your puppy's digestive system, you should feed it the same food, on the same time schedule, that the breeder or pet shop manager used. When the puppy tires, pick it up and place it in its cage or sleeping box to rest. After a few days, the puppy will learn to seek out its sleeping area on its own.

You will know that your cocker has become confident and feels safe in its new bed when it begins to do what cocker owners call the "circle." In this behavior, which is believed to be inherited from the wild wolf, the dog walks in circles on its sleeping blanket several times before it curls up and falls asleep. One of my dogs, Fiver, earned his nickname by always circling his bed no fewer than five times before settling down for the night.

During its first day in your home, you can expect your puppy to take several short naps. It is unlikely, however, to sleep throughout the night. Usually the puppy will wake up and, finding itself in a dark and strange place, will begin to whine and whimper for its mother and siblings.

It is extremely important that you leave your puppy in its own bed and not be tempted to take it into yours. If you are using a cage, do not take the puppy out; otherwise, you will be teaching it to cry every time it wants to get out of its cage. The puppy must learn how to behave when it is alone, and it is best to start this lesson as early as possible. If you wish, you can try sitting next to your puppy's bed for a while, calming the little newcomer with soothing words, or petting it, but do not pick it up. When the puppy calms down, you can try going back to bed.

To ease some of the feelings of loneliness, you should spend part of the first day preparing for the long night to come. When your puppy looks tired, put it in its bed with a few toys. Draw the curtains and turn out the lights to make the room as dark as possible. Then leave the room, making sure that the puppy cannot get out and cannot see or hear you. Most likely, your puppy will begin to cry. If this happens, wait at least five minutes before returning. Should the puppy settle down, let at least ten minutes pass before reentering the room. Repeating this procedure several times during the day should help to lessen the feelings of isolation and alienation that your puppy will experience at night.

Home Alone

Don't leave your puppy alone for long periods of time for the first few days. In addition to the emotional stress an unsupervised puppy feels when left alone, it can get into a lot of trouble, some of which may be physically harmful. If you must leave, have a relative, neighbor, or close friend "puppy sit," preferably in your home. Taking your puppy to another strange place will only multiply its anxiety.

After a few weeks, when your cocker has begun to feel completely comfortable in your home, and has gained your trust and confidence, you can begin to leave it alone for longer and longer periods. Regardless of how confident you are, however, I advise you to limit your puppy's access to the portion of your home that contains its feeding and sleeping areas. Also, be sure to inspect these rooms again to be sure that no potential hazards are within your puppy's reach.

Grooming a Cocker Spaniel

The cocker spaniel possesses a dense, medium-length body coat with a certain amount of undercoating. Besides giving this breed a beautiful appearance, the cocker's coat offers it protection against the elements. To fulfill these two functions, the coat must be kept in top condition. Cockers also possess long, feathered hair on their ears, chest, abdomen, and legs, which must be properly

Caring for a Cocker Spaniel

groomed to prevent snarls and matting. To keep your cocker in show condition, your regimen should consist of a good brushing every two or three days (daily when your dog is shedding its seasonal coat) and a thorough grooming once every two weeks.

Equipment

The following is a list of the grooming equipment that every cocker owner should have: a comb, a slicker brush, a pin brush, shears, nail clippers, ear cleaning solution, and cotton swabs. Many people also find it to their advantage to have electric trimmers and a wide variety of combs, brushes, and shears. While this extra equipment is considered mandatory for professional groomers and handlers, the average dog owner may have trouble justifying the additional cost.

If you are lax in your regular grooming regimen, your spaniel's coat can quickly become snarled and tangled, much like this dog's. If your pet proves to be an unwilling client, you may want to consider purchasing a grooming table, which comes with restraining harnesses.

Finally, no matter how experienced you become at grooming your cocker, it is a good idea to keep a small bottle of styptic powder handy, in case of accidents that may cause bleeding.

Regular Brushing

Start by using the slicker brush to thoroughly brush the dog's back and sides, avoiding all the areas of the body that have longer hair. Then use the pin brush for all the feathering on the legs, abdomen, chest, and ears. When brushing, take particular care to remove stubborn tangles and matted areas. Once the brushing is completed, comb the entire coat to remove all loose hairs.

While brushing, look for signs of fleas and ticks. If you see any, treat your cocker with a spray or powder immediately. The longer you wait, the faster these pests can multiply and the harder it becomes to remove them all. If you notice any unusual skin conditions, seek the advice of your veterinarian.

During these regular sessions, you should give special attention to your cocker's ears. Like most long-eared breeds, cockers are prone to ear trouble. To avoid serious infections, you should trim

For severe tangles and matted hair, try using some detangling lotion or spray before you begin the grooming process.

out all excess hair from around the ear canals and carefully remove any wax buildup, using a commercial ear-cleaning solution and cotton swabs. A pair of tweezers is handy to remove any loose hairs that have gotten into the ear. You should use the utmost care when probing around your dog's sensitive ear canals. In fact, I would advise novices to ask a professional groomer or a veterinarian to demonstrate the proper way to clean a cocker's ears before they try it themselves. Careless probing into a dog's ears can cause severe damage.

The Thorough Grooming

Thorough grooming should begin with your regular brushing and combing procedure. Next, with a sharp pair of shears remove all straggly hairs and trim back any overfeathered areas. The pictures and illustrations in this book will provide

Electric clippers can speed up the grooming process, but they must be used correctly. Be sure to hold the clipper with the blades parallel to the dog's skin. Never dig the cutting edge into the skin.

When trimming, it is important to move the clippers in the proper direction. Clip down the folds at the side of the neck (top left). Clip hair away from around the ear canal (top right). Clip the excess hair above the ears and behind the head toward the top of the skull (bottom left). Clip the hair on the back with downward motions (bottom right).

excellent visual advice as to how long and full your cocker's coat should be. When clipping, try to maintain a smooth blending of the coat as it goes from head to neck to shoulders and chest, and continue on to the tail and hind legs.

After trimming the coat, check the bottoms of your dog's paws and cut the hair between the pads as short as possible. This will reduce the chance of infection due to damp weather, as well as improving your dog's traction.

Another important part of your cocker's "paw care" is to trim its nails. If your cocker is an active, outdoor dog, you may not need to trim its nails very often. However, the nails of the average house dog can grow back rather quickly. Before you try to trim your dog's nails, you should learn from an experienced groomer or a veterinarian how to use a pair of clippers. Improper use of this tool can cause your dog a great deal of pain. Each of your dog's nails has a blood vessel, called the "quick," which

Caring for a Cocker Spaniel

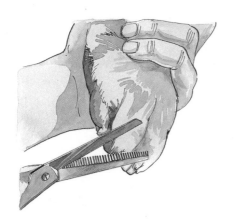

Using a pair of scissors, trim the excess hair from between the toes and the foot pads.

Clip your cocker's nails at an angle, making sure not to cut the quick.

runs through its center. You can see the quick when you examine the dog's claws. When trimming the nails, you must be careful not to cut the quick because it contains sensitive nerve endings. As your dog's claws grow longer, so does the quick.

The objective in clipping your dog's nails is to cut as close to the quick as possible. Routine pedicures will assure that you do not have to cut the quick to trim the nail to a comfortable length. If, however, you should accidentally cut the quick, it will bleed; the bleeding can be stopped by using a styptic powder. Cut the nails at an angle perpendicular to the growth of the quick, and let the dog's walking and running smooth the nail to the proper shape.

Tooth care is also an important part of grooming. An adequate supply of hard foods, such as biscuits and rawhide bones, can help prevent the buildup of tartar. Excessive tartar can lead to deterioration of the gums and tooth loss. Brushing your dog's teeth with a toothbrush, using baking soda or a commercial neutral baking soda toothpaste, as well as adding a little lemon juice or fresh tomatoes to the cocker's food, will also help to keep tartar in

check. If the buildup of tartar becomes extreme, it will have to be scraped off by your veterinarian.

As a final step in your grooming procedure, check your dog's eyes and clean out any sticky discharge that has accumulated in the corners. Because of the sensitivity of the eyes, this procedure too should be learned from a professional groomer or your veterinarian. As a breed, cockers suffer from various eye problems, which are described in detail in the chapter entitled "Ailments and Illnesses."

When checking the eyes, you must avoid putting your fingers too close to the sensitive eyeballs. If you gently pull back on the skin above the eyebrow and below the eye, you can expose enough of the area to observe it safely.

Bathing Your Cocker

In general, bathing should be thought of as a last resort. While shampooing your dog's coat may help eliminate dirt and "doggie odors," it is also likely to remove much of the natural oils that make

Caring for a Cocker Spaniel

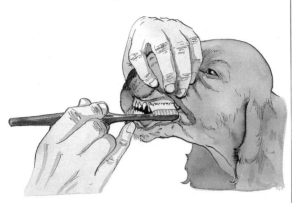

Once a week, use a toothbrush topped with baking soda to prevent the formation of tartar on your cocker's teeth.

When a bath becomes necessary, be sure to use a high-quality shampoo, and work it in thoroughly to get out all the grime and dirt.

Two completely different looks. (Top) With the coat hand-stripped and thoroughly brushed, this dog is ready for bench competitions. (Bottom) The clipped and brushed coat of this cocker is more practical for hot summer weather, as well as for competition in the field or obedience ring.

the coat weatherproof. Excessive bathing will also tend to dry out your cocker's skin and promote excessive shedding. Whenever possible, therefore, clean dirt from your dog's coat with a wet, slightly soapy cloth.

If a bath becomes necessary, use a high-quality shampoo and be sure to rinse it completely from the dog's coat; soap residue can irritate your cocker's skin. Dry your dog by rubbing it briskly with a towel. If you wish to accelerate the drying process, you can use a hot-air dryer. Once most of the water has been removed, you should brush and comb out the coat. Keep your dog indoors and away from drafts until it is completely dry.

In particular, try to avoid giving a puppy a bath until it is at least six months old or until it has had its permanent vaccinations. Puppies are particularly susceptable to drafts and can become sick after being soaked to the skin. However, should the puppy's coat become heavily soiled with oily dirt or excrement, a bath may become necessary. In this case, be sure to dry the coat thoroughly and to keep the puppy in a warm, draft-free location for several hours afterward.

Caring for a Cocker Spaniel

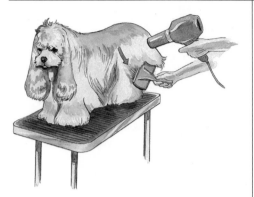

A hot-air blow dryer can speed up the drying process. Continue brushing the dog while using the dryer in order to get out all the water and to prevent the coat from becoming "frizzled."

Lifting and Carrying a Cocker Spaniel

To prevent injuries, be sure that everyone in your family, as well as visitors, learns how to lift and carry your puppy. The proper technique requires that one hand be under the puppy's chest, while the other hand is placed behind the dog to support its rear end and hindlegs. Never pick a puppy up by the scruff of the neck or with one hand under its abdomen. Both of these methods can hurt the dog.

There are few times when it is necessary to carry an adult cocker. You should avoid pampering your dog by carrying it up a flight of stairs or outside to its run. Let your cocker get as much exercise as it can, and lift and carry it only when absolutely necessary. If you find that you must lift your adult cocker, you should do it in much the same fashion as you would a puppy, that is, with one hand under the chest and the other supporting the hindquarters.

You should be warned that cockers sometimes fake injuries in order to get picked up and given extra attention or to avoid doing things that they do

The proper way to hold your puppy. Supporting its rear and hindquarters with one hand, support its chest with the other.

not want to do. My parents have told me of a dog with this habit that they owned when I was an infant.

Whenever my father was working outdoors, the dog, Sable (named for her color), would be allowed to run through the woods or across the yard. As soon as my mother would come outside to check on things, Sable would stop in midstride, "limp" over to my mother, and give a little whimper. Naturally, my mother would get all excited, pick up her four-legged "baby," and bestow lavish petting and reassuring words. As soon as my mother went back indoors, however, Sable would begin to run freely again. I have been told this act went on for many years. Strangely enough, Sable never "limped" for my father. I guess she knew that the trick would not get the same results from him.

Should your dog truly become injured or sick and need to be taken to the veterinarian, you will be well advised to put on the dog's muzzle before moving the animal. A dog that is in severe pain may act unpredictably, and may snap at or bite anyone who tries to help it. Once the threat of biting has been eliminated, you can lift the dog by placing one arm between both the front and the rear pair of legs and resting the dog's head in the crook of your arm, thereby keeping it from falling forward. You can also move an injured dog by placing it on its side on a blanket, which can serve as a stretcher.

On The Road Again—Traveling with and without Your Cocker Spaniel

Many people consider their dogs to be members of their family; as such, they are always taken on family trips and vacations. If you are such a person, and wish to take your cocker wherever you go, a little planning is all it takes to make everything go smoothly.

Nowadays your dog can travel by air, rail, sea, or car. Depending on your mode of transportation, you should contact your airline, railroad, or cruise line to see whether it can accommodate your pet. Some carriers will even supply a suitably sized shipping crate to house your cocker.

You will be happy to know that just about all major airlines and major railroads operating within the United States accept dogs. It is more difficult, however, to find transportation if you are traveling abroad because each foreign country has its own set of regulations, and many carriers are not equipped to meet these regulations. Should you find a form of transportation that will accept your cocker, be sure you check out the costs and the rules regarding pets ahead of time.

If you are planning to travel abroad, you should obtain a copy of the rules pertaining to pets from the consulate of the country you will visit. While most countries have minimal requirements, others have quarantine regulations and rules regarding vaccinations and health certificates which you must obtain from a licensed veterinarian.

When traveling by car, it is best to keep your dog in its cage. Driving is difficult enough without worrying about what your dog is up to. When driving, open the window enough to give your dog fresh air, but be careful not to expose it to drafts, which can cause eye, ear, and respiratory problems. Make a rest stop at least every two hours, and walk your dog on a leash, giving it ample time to relieve itself. Since the inside of a car can become very hot, allow your dog to drink regularly. Keep its water in a bottle on the floor of the car, where it will remain cool. If your dog tends to get carsick, you should obtain tablets for motion sickness from your veterinarian.

When packing for your cocker, be sure to include its grooming equipment, food and water dishes, leash, muzzle, cage, blanket, and, if possible, enough food to last the entire trip. Travel will probably cause additional stress to your dog's digestive system. By feeding your pet the type of food it is accustomed to, you can help to minimize digestive upsets.

If you choose not to take your dog when you travel, I recommend having a friend or relative look after it. Optimally, the "dogsitter" will come to your house whenever necessary. In this way, your dog can stay in a familiar environment. If you cannot find a trustworthy person to take care of your cocker, the breeder or pet store manager from whom you purchased the dog may be willing to look after it while you are away. If this is not feasible, you will have to resort to a boarding kennel. Before you decide, however, inspect the kennel to make sure that it is clean and well managed, and that the proprietor can and will meet your cocker's special needs.

Whatever arrangements you make, you should be aware that cocker spaniels can be very temperamental and do not always take well to being away from their masters for long periods of time. You would be amazed at how often a cocker owner returning from a trip is bombarded with the sitter's "dog-from-hell" stories. In very short order, however, you will find that your pet is once again its sweet, loving self.

Nutrition

What Do I Feed My Dog?

The nutritional requirements of dogs have probably not changed very much since the time when these animals were first domesticated. Our understanding of these needs, however, has increased greatly in recent years, thanks to advances in scientific research. In fact, the National Research Council (NRC), a division of the National Academy of Science of the United States, has compiled and interpreted vast quantities of data and has published an almost complete study entitled the "Nutrient Requirements of Dogs." This report establishes the minimun amount of every nutrient needed to maintain the health of the average adult dog, as well as the requirements of growing puppies.

This NRC study is used by practically every company that manufactures commercial dog foods, to help it formulate its products. In fact, for a dog food to be certified as "complete" in the United States, it must meet or exceed all the nutritional requirements established by the NRC and must pass actual feeding tests on dogs.

A complete commercial dog food wil provide your pet with balanced amounts of protein, fat, carbohydrates, vitamins, minerals, and trace elements. These nutrients may be added directly into the formula or contained in other ingredients that are used.

Scientifically, dogs are classified as carnivores, that is, meat-eaters. They have the ability, however, to effectively utilize a remarkably wide variety of foodstuffs to meet their nutritional needs. Thus, if you were to read the ingredient listings on several different dog foods, you might notice large variations. It is therefore very difficult to determine which food is best for your dog. To help you decide, I recommend that you seek the advice of your breeder and your veterinarian. Your breeder will know what food has worked best for your dog's dam (mother), as well as other cockers, while your veterinarian will have a working knowledge of dog foods based on the experiences of other clients. A veterinarian will also be able to recommend a special diet should your cocker's health dictate the need for one.

As you can probably guess by now, I strongly urge all dog owners to use high quality commercial dog foods. When preparing a dog's food from scratch, it becomes all too easy to give your pet either too much or too little of an essential nutrient. This process is also much more time consuming and significantly more expensive. If, however, you feel that you want to prepare your dog's food fresh, as an act of love, I strongly recommend that you read as many books as you can find on animal nutrition and also seek the advice of your veterinarian.

Types of Commercial Dog Food

Dry Dog Foods: These are the most popular type of dog food. They can be pellets, kibbles, extruded shapes, or whole biscuits. As the name implies, dry foods are low in moisture content (usually about 10 to 12 percent). They contain mostly grains, cereal by-products, animal and soybean meals, and fats, as well as vitamin and mineral supplements.

Semimoist Dog Foods: These foods are moderate in moisture content (between 25 and 30 percent) and contain much the same ingredients as dry foods, but usually with less meat meal and more whole meat. Semimoist foods are usually formed into patties or simulated meat chunks.

Canned Dog Foods: These foods are usually very high in moisture (sometimes as much as 75 percent). Some canned foods are nutritionally complete, while others are made to add to dry dog foods to make the latter more palatable. Thus, when buying canned foods, you should be extra careful in your selection.

No matter what type of commercial dog food you choose, be sure to read the label carefully for nutritional information and feeding tips.

When feeding a puppy, use a flat dish with low sides that give easier access to the food.

Special Foods: Advances in animal health research have led to the development of commercial dog foods designed to supply complete nutrition during every phase of your dog's life. In addition to puppy foods, you can now find special diets for active dogs, inactive dogs, overweight dogs, and older dogs. Some companies even make special diets for dogs with medical problems such as heart conditions and kidney disorders. (These special medical diets are available only from your veterinarian.)

Food for the Finicky Dog: In general, cocker spaniels are not finicky eaters. However, an occasional dog will not eat the food that the breeder or veterinarian recommends. If you happen to get such a cocker, and you are using a dry dog food, you might try adding some canned "all-meat" dog food to the diet. If this does not work, you may have to try several types of foods before you find one the dog will eat.

Feeding Table Scraps

Many people feel that they must give their precious pooches samplings from their own nightly banquets. Be warned that this practice has great potential for teaching your cocker some bad habits, such as begging. If, despite my warning, you must share your meal, at least give your dog the right types of scraps.

To avoid trichinosis, never feed your cocker pork that is not completely cooked. Trichinosis is a condition that is caused by a parasite sometimes found in pigs; this parasite can be destroyed by thorough cooking of the meat.

Also avoid feeding your dog pieces of chicken that have bones in them. Chicken bones are very soft and tend to splinter into sharp pieces when chewed. If swallowed, these splinters can cut, or get lodged in, your dog's mouth, throat, or digestive tract. In short, if you must feed your dog a real meat bone (even though dog biscuits and rawhide bones make excellent substitutes), make sure that it is a good, solid, well-cooked beef or pork bone.

Cockers, like most dogs, have a strong hereditary urge to hide or bury bones and other food scraps or treats for use during times of need. Do not be surprised, therefore, if your cocker tries to take its bones outdoors so that it can bury them in your yard. Of course, if the urge is strong enough and the dog is prevented from taking food outside, a clever cocker may find other places—perhaps under carpets or furniture, or in a dark corner or closet—to build up its larder.

Since old food can give off quite an odor, I suggest that you allow a dog with a strong desire to store food to bury an occasional bone in the backyard. Better this than to have your cocker resurrect an old meal while you are entertaining guests.

Importance of Water

Of all the nutrients in a high quality diet, there is none more imporant than water. Water is vital to every living cell and comprises nearly 60 percent of your dog's body weight. Unlike some other animals, dogs cannot store much water and must constantly replenish whatever they lose; you must, therefore, always provide your dog with an adequate supply.

A cocker's water intake will depend on several factors, including the air temperature, the type of food the animal eats, the amount of exercise it gets, and its temperament. You should avoid giving your dog very cold water, especially after strenuous exercise.

Special Considerations in Feeding Your Cocker

While the NRC study provides the minimum nutrient requirements of growing and adult dogs, several additional factors may affect the type and quantity of nutrients that an individual animal may need. Exercise, metabolism rate, individual growth rate, the kind of work it does, and many environmental factors all influence the quantity of food your dog requires.

In general, as a dog becomes older and less active, it needs less food (or fewer calories from its food) and can become overweight if its requirements have changed but its diet has not. You should therefore watch your dog's weight and change its food intake as necessary.

Coat condition is often another good indicator of the adequacy of your dog's diet. A dry coat and flaky skin may signify a fat, fatty acid, or vitamin deficiency. This condition is often accompanied by scratching and is many times misdiagnosed by the dog owner as external parasites or other skin ailments. The proper diet should produce a soft, shiny coat, rich in color.

Cockers that get a lot of exercise, are used for hunting, or participate in numerous field and obedience trials will usually require a diet that is higher in calories. The same is true for dogs that spend a lot of time outdoors in cold weather; such dogs need about 50 percent more calories than their counterparts in a warm climate. Once again, body weight and coat condition are the best indicators of how well your dog's diet meets the animal's needs.

If for any reason you suspect that your dog's food is not providing adequate nourishment, you should seek the advice of your veterinarian. It may be that a change in diet is needed, or a medical problem may require attention.

A final note on feeding a dog: You should know that dogs do not require a wide variety of foods and will not tire of eating the same thing every day. If you feed your cocker a high-quality, well-balanced diet, it can thrive on this food for its entire life. If, however, your dog is not eating properly, a physical or emotional problem may have arisen. Therefore, if your cocker refuses to eat and falls off its diet for two or three days, you should take it to your veterinarian for an examination.

Ailments and Illnesses

In General

Dogs, like humans, are subject to a wide variety of illnesses. While the cocker spaniel is no exception, you will be glad to know that there are several things you can do to prevent most of the ailments described in this chapter.

Proper nutrition, good hygiene, and an adequate exercise program are essential in keeping your cocker healthy. By providing these requisites, combined with scheduled visits to the veterinarian for booster shots and routine examinations, you can help your cocker to live a long and healthy life. You must never underestimate the importance of keeping scheduled appointments with your veterinarian. Early detection is the key in preventing many problems from getting out of hand, and it sometimes takes a trained medical eye to detect early symptoms.

Although the descriptions in this chapter of some of the ailments may be graphic, they are not meant to scare you into keeping your dog isolated in a sterilized room. Instead, my purpose is to help you to understand the symptoms of illnesses and to recognize the importance of vaccinations and of routine veterinary examinations.

What Are Symptoms?

Simply put, symptoms are indicators of diseases or disorders; and because dogs cannot talk, symptoms provide the only means whereby you can infer that your pet is not feeling well. Some symptoms are very specific and indicate the presence of a single illness, while others are common to a wide variety of problems. Although understanding the symptoms or combinations of symptoms associated with certain ailments may help you narrow down the possibilities, the trained eye of a veterinarian is usually required to determine the exact cause.

There are several symptoms of which every dog owner should be aware. If you notice any one, or a combination of them, you should call your veterinarian. Be alert for physical exhaustion, loss of appetite or of thirst, excessive appetite or thirst, unusual sneezing or wheezing, excessive coughing, runny nose, discharge from the eyes or ears, poor coat condition, foul breath, blood in the stool, slight paralysis, limping, trembling or shaking, swelling or lumps on the body, sudden weight loss, cloudy or orange-colored urine, inability to urinate, uncontrolled urination, moaning or whimpering, unusual slobbering or salivation, vomiting, and diarrhea.

The last two, vomiting and diarrhea, are probably the most common of all canine symptoms. However, they do not always indicate the presence of a serious ailment. For instance, it is not uncommon for a recent mother to instinctively regurgitate her food in an attempt to feed her puppies. Likewise, young dogs sometimes attack their food with such gusto that their natural defensive mechanisms send the food back up again. (This behavior usually subsides as the dog matures.) Extremely nervous dogs may also regurgitate food if they become frightened. A dog may even eat some grass and subsequently vomit in a voluntary attempt to purge its digestive tract. This purging behavior, however, may also indicate a larger problem.

Persistent vomiting, on the other hand, should be reported to your veterinarian immediately. It can be caused by several digestive disorders and diseases, and is often accompanied by irregular bowel movements, such as diarrhea.

The occasional soft stool, by itself, is usually nothing to worry about. During warm weather, when dogs tend to drink more water, their stools may become loose or they may get diarrhea. Diarrhea may also be caused by minor stomach upsets. You can help clear up the occasional attack of diarrhea by regulating your cocker's diet. Add thoroughly cooked starches such as rice and oatmeal to its food, and eliminate milk, broth, and similar liquids. Be sure, however, to keep the dog's water dish full of clean, cool water.

Continuous or frequent watery bowel movements, on the other hand, indicate a serious ailment and should be brought to the attention of your veterinarian. If left untreated, severe diarrhea can cause dehydration and other problems.

Preventive Medicine

As a conscientious dog owner, you will be responsible for establishing an effective health plan for your cocker. Diet, exercise, and hygiene are all important factors in maintaining your dog's physical well-being. Your cocker's mental health will also depend on you and your ability to establish a proper dog/master relationship. If all of these elements are incorporated into your daily routine, you will have laid the foundation of a strong preventive health system. This system can become complete, however, only through the inclusion of vaccinations and booster shots against infectious diseases. For these you must take your dog to your veterinarian.

Six Infectious Diseases Requiring Immunizations

Before the discovery of vaccines, several infectious diseases ran rampant through the canine population, leading to large numbers of deaths. Most of these diseases are caused by bacteria or viruses that dogs can contract from a wide variety of sources. Advances in modern medical science have led to the development of vaccines that can protect dogs against all the major infectious diseases. However, while vaccines are extremely effective, not all of them offer permanent protection. Thus, booster shots may be required from time to time.

There are six infectious diseases against which your cocker should be immunized: rabies, canine distemper, canine hepatitis, parvovirus, kennel cough, and leptospirosis. Chances are that your breeder will have had your puppy vaccinated before you get it. However, three to four weeks are required for the first group of immunizations to become completely effective. When you pick up your puppy, your breeder or pet shop manager can supply you with a copy of the dog's medical records, which will indicate the dates of treatment and will also remind you when your dog will need booster shots. To be safe, keep the puppy away from all nonimmunized animals until the vaccines can take full effect.

Rabies: This viral infection, one of the most dangerous dog diseases, attacks the victim's nervous system and can be transmitted to all warm-blooded animals, including humans. While normally transmitted through a bite, this disease can also be contracted if the saliva of the infected animal comes into contact with an open wound.

In its early stages a rabies-infected dog may exhibit behavioral changes. A normally friendly animal may act extremely irritable one minute and

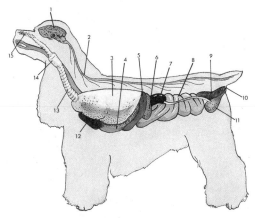

Internal organs of the cocker spaniel

1. brain	6. spleen	11. bladder
2. spinal cord	7. kidney	12. heart
3. lungs	8. small intestine	13. trachea
4. liver	9. colon	14. thyroid cartilage
5. stomach	10. anus	15. sinus cavity

be back to normal the next. As the disease progresses, the symptoms include a loss of appetite, frequent urination, and attempts to eat or bite foreign objects such as wood or stones. Later symptoms include paralysis of the face and throat, which causes the dog to drool excessively and makes swallowing difficult. During this stage the dog may also become more vicious, thereby greatly increasing the chance of spreading the disease. Eventually the paralysis becomes so severe that the victim cannot eat or drink, and dies shortly thereafter.

The rabies vaccine will not save an unvaccinated dog that is infected by a rabid animal; therefore, all dogs need to be immunized against the disease, with booster shots given every three years. Because this disease can be transmitted to humans, all rabies incidents are considered public health hazards and should be reported. If you suspect any stray dog or other animal in your neighborhood of having rabies, you should notify the public health authorities immediately.

Canine Distemper: This highly contagious viral disease was once second to rabies in respect to its danger to dogs; today, however, dogs that are vaccinated against it will not contract it easily. Canine distemper is spread through the urine, feces, saliva, and even nasal discharges of the infected animal. The virus may also be carried on blankets, brushes, and clothing.

The early stages of this disease are characterized by fever, diarrhea, depression, a dry cough, and watery discharges from the eyes and nose. Advanced symptoms may include a loss of equilibrium, cramps, twitching of leg and facial muscles, convulsive seizures, and partial paralysis.

Canine distemper is almost always fatal to a young dog that has not been immunized. In older dogs the disease can cause damage to the central nervous system. If a puppy's mother was properly vaccinated, she is able to passively immunize her offspring by passing antibodies (proteins that attack diseases) to her young through her milk. Such immunization lasts throughout the nursing period.

After weaning, however, the puppies will need additional vaccinations. Once a dog contracts canine distemper, it can be very difficult to treat. Thus, the only effective protection against this disease is vaccination and booster shots.

Canine Hepatitis: This contagious viral disease, which attacks primarily the liver and gastrointestinal tract, should not be confused with human hepatitis. This disease is spread throughout the canine population in much the same way as canine distemper. Canine hepatitis cannot be contracted by humans; however, they can carry the disease on their clothing. Dogs that have been vaccinated against this disease rarely contract it. Older dogs that contract the disease can sometimes be saved, but it is almost always fatal to unvaccinated puppies.

Symptoms of canine hepatitis include diarrhea, fever, severe thirst, lethargy, inflammation of the nasal passages, and liver inflammation, which makes the abdomen sensitive to the touch. To relieve the pain in the liver and stomach, dogs with canine hepatitis may arch their backs and rub their bellies on the floor. This disease develops extremely rapidly. Affected dogs may appear healthy one day and very ill the next.

Parvovirus: This disease began to appear in dogs only in the last few decades; two forms are now known. One type causes inflammation of the heart muscles of very young puppies, and infected animals quickly collapse and die of heart complications. The other, more common form, is called parvoviral enteritis. It is characterized by constant vomiting of a foamy yellow-brown liquid and bloody, foul-smelling diarrhea. These symptoms result in severe fluid loss, which can lead to dehydration and death in a few days. Patting the undersides of an infected dog will cause it to wince in pain. Parvoviral enteritis can occur in dogs of all ages. Both forms of the virus are carried and transmitted in much the same way as canine distemper.

Puppies should be vaccinated against parvovirus before their fourteenth week. Immunization against the virus must be repeated frequently in order to be effective; yearly booster shots are recommended. If the disease is detected early enough, an unvaccinated dog can sometimes be saved by lengthy, painful, and expensive treatments. Clearly, immunization is by far the better alternative.

Kennel Cough: The term refers to viral and/or bacterial infections that affect the upper respiratory tract of dogs. The disease agents, which cause inflammation of the trachea and bronchi, are common whenever and wherever dogs congregate. If you are planning to board your dog in a kennel, therefore, be sure that your pet is vaccinated against these diseases. Yearly booster shots are recommended.

Leptospirosis: This disease is caused by bacteria that are transmitted through the urine of rats, mice, or infected dogs. A dog can contract the disease only through ingestion. Leptospirosis attacks an infected dog's liver and kidneys and is extremely painful.

The symptoms of this disease may be very similar to those of canine distemper and canine hepatitis. However, leptospirosis usually causes a kidney infection, which changes the color and odor of the urine. The urine of an infected dog often has a deep yellow to orange color and a strong offensive odor.

Leptospirosis can be transmitted to humans by unvaccinated animals. Vaccinations against this disease are the only way to protect your dog, yourself, and your family. If not treated in its early stages, leptospirosis is almost always fatal to dogs.

Vaccination Schedule

Temporary Immunizations: Starting at four to six weeks of age, the passive immunity that a puppy receives from its mother's milk begins to wear off. At this point you must take your puppy to the veterinarian for its vaccinations. Your veterinarian will administer a series of immunizations to guard against distemper, canine hepatitis, par-

vovirus, kennel cough, and leptospirosis. Then you will have to return every three or four weeks until the puppy is four months old, so that it can receive the necessary booster shots. Antirabies vaccinations are usually not given until the puppy reaches the age of four months.

Booster Shots: Your veterinarian will explain the frequency for each type of booster, which ranges from six months for parvovirus to three years for rabies. Booster shots will provide your cocker with the maximum protection against these infectious diseases.

Shots before Mating: A female cocker that is to be bred should be brought to the veterinarian before her "season." It is important for her to receive booster shots so that she can adequately supply her puppies with the passive immunity they need. You should also bring a stool sample so that she can be checked for worms and treated if necessary.

Internal Parasites

Worms are by far the most common internal parasite of dogs. Most worms live in the digestive tract of the infected animal, and their eggs can be found in the dog's stool. To the untrained eye, all of these eggs look the same. Therefore, if you suspect your dog has worms, you will have to take a stool sample to your veterinarian so that the eggs or newly hatched larvae can be properly identified. Positive identification of the type of worm infestation is needed because most worming medications are not considered broad-spectrum, and they work only against one or two different families of worms. Your veterinarian will know exactly what medicine to administer to clear up any problem you encounter.

Although there is a wide variety of worms that may infest members of the canine family, most are very rare. Only the most common types are described in detail in this section.

Ailments and Illnesses

Roundworms: These parasites are white, are cylindrical, and can grow up to 4 inches (10 cm) long. The adult roundworms live in a dog's intestinal tract; there they embed themselves and their eggs, which are excreted in the dog's stool. If the eggs are then ingested by another animal, they will grow into adults in their new host, thus continuing the cycle.

While roundworms are rarely harmful to an adult dog, a heavy infestation can be fatal to a puppy. Since roundworms can be passed from a pregnant mother to her puppies, be sure to have your female's stool checked before mating her.

Symptoms of roundworm infestation include diarrhea, cramps, irregular appetite, weakness, bloated belly, and, in severe cases, paralysis. In addition, the infested dog's anus may itch, in which case the dog will squat down and skid its rump across the floor in an attempt to relieve the itch.

Tapeworms: These parasites also live in a dog's intestinal tract. The most common source of tapeworm is fleas, which act as carriers of the

Life cycle of the tapeworm. Tapeworm segments containing eggs are passed in a dog's feces. There they are ingested by fleas, which are in turn ingested by the same dog or others.

worm's eggs. When the flea is ingested by a biting dog, the eggs can begin to grow in its intestines.

The head of this worm has a series of hooks and suckers that it uses to attach itself tenaciously to the dog's small intestine. The body of the tapeworm grows in a long, segmented chain, with the tail section containing many eggs. On occasion, the worm will release the egg-containing section, which will then be passed in the dog's stool. These segments look like grains of rice and often stick to the hairs surrounding the dog's anus.

The symptoms of tapeworm infestation may take a long time to develop. Once they show themselves, they are similar to those caused by roundworm.

Heartworm: These parasites are prevalent only in certain areas. Infestations can be very serious and, if not treated promptly, even fatal. Heartworms attach themselves to the right side of the dog's heart and part of the lungs. They cause the heart to work harder, age rapidly, and eventually weaken.

Heartworms are transmitted by mosquitoes, which carry the worms' larvae. When a dog is bitten by these mosquitoes, the larvae can enter its bloodstream. About six months are required for the larvae to develop into mature heartworms.

Two drugs are used to prevent heartworms. One is Ivermectin; the other, diethylcarbamazine. Ivermectin is considered the drug of choice because it can be administered once a month, while diethylcarbamazine must be given daily throughout the mosquito season. Both of these drugs are available through your veterinarian. If you live in an area where heartworm is known to occur, you should have your dog tested annually before the

Cocker puppies love to run (top) and roughhouse (bottom left) with each other—but after a good workout, it's time to rest (bottom right).

Ailments and Illnesses

Life cycle of the heartworm. Mosquitoes carry the larvae and pass them into the dog's bloodstream. The larvae seek out the dog's heart and grow there.

mosquito season, as both of the drugs used to prevent the disease can be extremely harmful to an already-infested dog.

External Parasites

Fleas: The most common canine parasites, fleas cause more pain and suffering to dogs than any other ailment. They differ from other parasites in that they can jump a great distance from one dog to another. Fleas crawl under a dog's thick coat, biting and sucking its blood and causing severe itching. By scratching, the dog may develop eczema. You may find fleas very difficult to eliminate.

Cockers, for the most part, will get along well with other pets. Top: These two young companions probably will grow up together as friends. Bottom: Although this puppy seems friendly, the cat appears a little apprehensive. These two will have to be watched carefully before they can be left together unsupervised.

Buy a flea spray or powder in your pet store. Test the product by treating only a small area of your cocker's body. If the dog exhibits the signs of an allergic reaction, such as excessive salivation, foaming at the mouth, coughing, or wheezing, use a wet towel to clean the treated area immediately. If no reaction occurs, treat the entire dog as directed on the label. Be sure to cover the dog's eyes and nose with your hand while spraying, for both sprays and powders can irritate the mucous membranes. You must also disinfect all the areas where your dog may have caught the fleas, including its kennel and run, its blanket and sleeping box, and your furniture and carpets if your dog has any contact with them.

Ticks: These dangerous, bloodsucking parasites can be found in just about all countries worldwide. The danger lies in the fact that some species of ticks carry diseases.

The *brown dog tick* is large enough to see with the human eye. Although not all brown ticks are dangerous, this tick has been implicated as a carrier of such diseases as Rocky Mountain spotted fever and babesiosis. These two diseases have similar symptoms. In dogs, these diseases cause fever, anorexia, depression, lethargy, and a rapid pulse rate.

The *deer tick*, much smaller than the brown dog tick, is barely perceptible to the human eye. Deer ticks have recently become more widespread throughout the country and are no longer limited to the northeastern region of the United States. They are a potential health threat because they may carry Lyme disease, named after the Connecticut town where the ailment was first diagnosed in humans. The symptoms of this disease are stiffness, pain, fever, rashes, and inflammation of the joints. If diagnosed early enough, Lyme disease can be cured with antibiotic therapy.

In recent years, cases of tick-borne diseases have been on the rise, probably because an increasing number of host animals (mice, raccoons, deer, and opossums, to name a few) have moved into areas where previously they were scarce. Ticks breed on the animal they have infected and then leave it, seeking a new host such as a dog or a human.

Although humans cannot "catch" a tick-borne disease from an infected dog, they can become infected if bitten by the tick that is transmitting the disease. It is impossible to eradicate ticks from all areas, but you should keep your dog away from areas known to be tick-infested, such as open fields and woods. It is also a good practice to inspect the dog for ticks each time your cocker returns to the house. Be sure to check inside the ears and between the toes, as these areas are preferred by ticks. If your dog shows signs of any tick-borne disease, take your pet to your veterinarian immediately.

When a tick gets onto a dog, it will embed its head in the dog's skin and hold on fiercely. To remove a tick, first wash the infected area with alcohol, which helps to loosen the tick's grasp. When you have loosened the tick somewhat, place a pair of tweezers squarely over its head, as close to the dog's skin as possible. Lift the tick off the dog, being careful not to pull the parasite apart; if the head remains under the skin, it can cause infection. Once the tick has been removed, it can be destroyed by immersing it in a dilute solution of detergent or bleach. If you live in an area where tick-borne diseases are known to occur and you suspect the tick of being a carrier, place it in a tightly sealed jar, and bring it to your veterinarian for examination.

Lice: Like all other external parasites, lice burrow into one area, suck blood, and cause irritation. If your dog is infested, you can see clusters of eggs on its hairs. Lice can be very dangerous, so bring your dog to a veterinarian promptly if you spot eggs. He or she can eliminate the lice by using an insecticide dip.

Mites: These very small parasites do their damage by burrowing into a dog's skin, causing intense itching. Mites are no bigger than a pinhead;

but when they burrow into the skin in large numbers, they can cause a serious skin disease called mange. Fortunately, mange rarely occurs in healthy dogs kept in a clean environment. The condition is typically found in dogs that frequent unsanitary places and suffer from improper nutrition. There are two principal forms of mange that afflict dogs: sarcoptic mange and demodectic mange.

Sarcoptic mange is usually easier to recognize because it makes a dog more miserable and causes more scratching. The skin in the affected area becomes dry, thickened, wrinkled, and crusty. As the dog scratches, the area becomes red, completely void of hair, and full of bloody sores. As the mites breed and lay eggs, the mange will begin to spread. As the spreading continues, the dog will develop a foul body odor.

Demodectic mange is harder to detect because it may result only in slight hair loss and reddening and some inflammation of the skin. Likewise, it does not always cause a great deal of itching or irritation. Even though its symptoms are less noticeable, demodectic mange is usually harder to cure.

Your veterinarian can identify either form of mange by taking a skin scraping and examining it under a microscope. Once the type of mange is identified, proper treatment can begin.

Other Skin Disorders

Eczema: Symptoms such as red dots, pimples, damp spots, crusty and scaly skin, greasy skin, and a loss of hair may indicate that the dog has eczema. This general name is given to several different skin conditions. Eczema occurs in both wet and dry patches and may have many causes, including external parasites. Nutritional deficiencies, hormonal imbalances, excessive heat or dampness, and allergies can also cause these skin conditions. Usually, to cure an eczema problem, the specific cause must be found and treated.

One form of eczema that commonly afflicts cockers, however, has no known cause. This ailment results in the crusting or scaling of the skin on the dog's face, ears, trunk, and sometimes the entire body. Luckily it can be successfully treated with carefully measured doses of vitamin A. This therapy must be conducted under the supervision of a veterinarian, as excessive amounts of this vitamin may be harmful to the dog.

Ringworm: Another cause of skin problems is called ringworm. Ringworm is actually not a worm at all; it is a fungus that affects the outer layer of skin, hair, and nails. It may cause inflammation, itching, hair loss, and scabby areas. Certain forms of ringworm can be transmitted to humans, so prompt veterinarian treatment is essential. Should your dog be diagnosed as having ringworm, it would be advisable to have all humans who come into contact with the animal also examined and, if afflicted, treated at once.

Ear and Eye Disorders

This section should be of special interest to the cocker spaniel owner, because several ear and eye disorders are inherent in this breed.

Otitis: This ailment is common to most dogs that possess long, pendulous ears. Otitis occurs when a dog's ear care is neglected, and the buildup of moisture, dirt, wax, hair, and other foreign materials allows bacteria, yeasts, and molds to infect the external ears. The afflicted animal may hold one ear low (if only one ear is infected), scratch or rub the ear, shake its head, or cock its head at unusual angles. Often the ear will become reddened or inflamed, and sometimes there is a discharge of puslike fluid from the ear canal. Otitis can be extremely difficult for your veterinarian to treat, and in many cases the affected dog will need several retreatments. It is therefore wise, as a pre-

Regular cleaning is important in preventing ear problems, which may arise from wax and dirt buildup. If not removed, dirt and wax can provide a place for harmful bacteria to grow.

ventive measure, to make ear cleaning a regular part of your grooming schedule.

Distichiasis: This genetically linked eye disorder, which continues to plague cocker spaniels, is caused when some of the dog's eyelashes grow incorrectly and come into contact with the cornea. Distichiasis can cause squinting, excessive tearing, and inflammation. While electrolysis may be a temporary solution, surgery is usually required to correct the condition permanently.

Ectropion: Also a hereditary eye ailment in some cocker bloodlines, ectropion is characterized by an unusual growing or rolling out of the dog's lower eyelids. This condition allows eye discharge to accumulate in the folds, where it may cause conjunctivitis (an inflammation of the membrane that keeps the dog's eye moist). Ectropion also requires surgery to correct.

Glaucoma: Another ailment with a high incidence rate in cockers is glaucoma, caused by a fluid buildup that exerts abnormal pressure inside the eye. This tends to enlarge the eyeball, causing

Whenever you clean your cocker's eyes, you should examine them to be sure that they are moist and clear. Cloudiness may indicate cataracts or other ailments that should be reported immediately to your veterinarian.

much pain and possibly blindness. Glaucoma may be treated with drugs or by surgery but is sometimes imposssible to cure.

Retinal Dysplasia: This genetically linked eye ailment, which also affects cockers, is characterized by lesions on the retina, which reduce the dog's vision. Eventually the retina may become completely detached, causing blindness.

All of the hereditary eye ailments described above will cause your dog much pain and discomfort, or worse; and if treatable, they can cost you a lot of money. It is therefore worth your time to make sure that your breeder or pet shop manager has had all of his or her cockers checked for these defects before breeding them. It is also wise to take your cocker to your veterinarian for regular ocular examinations.

Other Health Problems

Constipation

Constipation occurs when solid waste products build up in a dog's digestive tract and cannot be passed easily. In most cases, constipation can be relieved by changing your cocker's diet and giving the dog a mild laxative. Half a cup of lukewarm milk every hour is usually very effective. You should also reduce the amount of dry bulk foods in your dog's diet until the stool is normal.

Constipation may also occur if a dog eats an indigestible object, such as a small toy or a stone. If you suspect that this has happened, contact your veterinarian immediately. Do not give a laxative if you suspect a foreign object. Surgery may be required.

Enteritis

Enteritis is a general term given to any inflammation of the intestinal tract. The condition can be caused by bacteria, poisons, worms, ulcer, swallowing foreign objects, change of diet, spicy foods, overexcitement, and so on. Symptoms may include diarrhea and foul-smelling stools; also, the dog may lie in contorted positions in an attempt to relieve the discomfort. If you notice these symptoms, contact your veterinarian immediately as professional care is usually required to cure this ailment.

Adding oatmeal cooked in water to the dog's food will alleviate the pain, without causing harm, until the cause can be identified. Also, the pectin in grated apples will offer relief to the cocker experiencing undiagnosed diarrhea.

Pneumonia and Other Respiratory Ailments

Dogs can contract many common throat and respiratory ailments, although they do not suffer from the common cold. These ailments are characterized by sneezing, coughing, runny nose, watery eyes, slight fever, and chills.

Pneumonia is usually caused by a primary virus that attacks the respiratory system: a secondary bacterial infection follows. Symptoms of pneumonia include coughing, shallow breathing, nasal discharge, loss of appetite, and fever. Pneumonia was once a common killer of dogs but, like most respiratory ailments, can now be successsfully treated with antibiotics, which can be administered by a veterinarian.

Hip Dysplasia

Hip dysplasia is a developmental disorder of the hip joints. It occurs most commonly in young dogs or larger breeds, but this inherited ailment has been known to plague cocker bloodlines. The condition itself is due to a hip-socket malformation that does not allow for the proper fit of the head of the femur.

At birth, the hip of the afflicted dog appears normal; signs of the disorder do not appear until the dog is at least five months old. The optimum age for a definite diagnosis is between 24 and 36 months. Hip dysplasia results in painful inflammation of the hip joint, which leads to permanent physical damage, including lameness and loss of the use of the back legs.

It is now possible for veterinarians to surgically correct the shape of the hip socket. Another surgical procedure, known as total hip replacement, has also been highly successful. Unfortunately, these procedures are performed only by a limited number of specialists, and they can be quite costly. Since this ailment is genetically linked, you must never breed a cocker with hip dysplasia.

Von Willebrand's Disease

Von Willebrand's disease is an inherited defect that is a form of hemophilia; the affected dog's blood does not clot as it should. All cockers should be tested for the presence of this ailment, and afflicted dogs should not be used for breeding. It is also important that your veterinarian know if your dog has a blood-clotting defect. If an afflicted dog becomes injured or requires surgery, the veterinarian will have to take special precautions. Depending on the type of defect and its severity, several treatment options are available. While the solution may be as simple as giving your dog oral

doses of vitamin K, expensive plasma transfusions may sometimes be needed.

Shock

Shock is a serious condition that results from a traumatic physical or emotional experience. The most common cause is an automobile accident. A dog in shock may appear to be asleep, or it may be semiconscious. Symptoms vary according to the severity of the condition. Breathing may be shallow, the dog's body may be cold, and its pulse may be rapid.

If your dog is in shock, try to calm it by speaking in a soft voice, pet it reassuringly, and, if possible, cover it with a blanket or an article of clothing. Because the actions of a dog in shock are unpredictable, however, use caution in handling it. Take it to a veterinarian immediately.

Broken Bones

Broken bones also frequently result from automobile accidents. A dog with a fracture will be in severe pain. Therefore, always approach an injured dog very carefully, as it may attempt to bite you. If

An injured or sick dog can act unpredictably and may bite. If necessary, you can make an emergency muzzle from a necktie or the soft belt of a bathrobe.

the dog has a compound fracture (the broken bone has punctured the skin), cover the wound with gauze or a clean cloth to help prevent infection, and bring the injured dog to a veterinarian as soon as possible. Any fracture, simple as well as compound, requires professional attention.

Poisoning

Although this section contains general information on poisoning, you should call directory assistance now and obtain the telephone number of the nearest poison control center. Keep this number easily accessible in case of emergency. If you know or suspect that your dog has ingested a specific poison, call the center for the proper antidote and then relay this information to your veterinarian. If you do not know what the dog has ingested, call your veterinarian and describe the symptoms.

Common symptoms of poisoning are stomach pains, howling, whimpering, vomiting, diarrhea, convulsions, tremors, and labored breathing. Many poisons are fatal if not treated quickly. If you know the type of poison, your veterinarian may be able to save your dog by inducing vomiting or diarrhea, by pumping its stomach, or by neutralizing the poison with appropriate medications.

False Pregnancy

In false pregnancy, the female behaves as if she were pregnant but is not. The affected dog may creep off by herself, run around restlessly, and paw at her bed. She may also carry toys, stuffed animals, or old shoes to her bed, and defend these objects as if they were puppies. She may even become overaggressive in protecting her "offspring."

Usually this condition disappears by itself, with the female returning to normal behavior. If it occurs several times a year, however, take your dog to your veterinarian. Although hormone therapy relieves the symptoms of false pregnancy, it is rarely recommended because it may cause further complications.

Your veterinarian may suggest surgical removal of the ovaries. This is safe, will spare your dog a great deal of pain, and may even prolong her life. Removal of the ovaries prevents recurrence of false pregnancy, which can lead to uterine infections. The surgery should not be performed while the symptoms are still apparent, however, because the protective behavior may then persist. It is best to postpone surgery until all symptoms have disappeared.

Nursing a Sick Dog

You should be able to perform several procedures if your dog becomes ill.

Taking the Temperature

The first procedure is taking your dog's temperature, for which you will need a regular rectal thermometer and some KY or petroleum jelly. The normal body temperature of an adult cocker spaniel is between 100.5 and 101.5°F (38 and 38.6°C). The temperature is slightly higher in younger dogs and slightly lower in older ones. If your dog is placid, simply shake the mercury below 100°F (37.7°C), lubricate the thermometer with the KY or petroleum jelly, slip the thermometer in, and keep it there for two or three minutes. If your dog resists, hold its head firmly in the crook of your arm, leaving your other arm free. Then insert the thermometer. A restless dog may have an elevated temperature of a degree or so; however, a markedly higher temperature is usually a cause for alarm.

This procedure will enable you to determine if the dog has either a fever or a below normal temperature (a symptom of poisoning). Wash the thermometer in cold water when you are done.

Taking the Pulse

You should also learn to take your dog's pulse. The best place to feel the pulse is the inside of the front paw or the inside of the thigh on the heart side. An adult cocker has a pulse rate of 75 to 95 beats per minute; in younger dogs the pulse is slightly quicker. In a calm, healthy dog the pulse is strong and steady.

A weak pulse may indicate poisoning; an irregular pulse is a symptom of fever or infection.

Administering Medication

Since it is extremely important that a sick dog take all of its prescribed medicine, you should also learn to administer medications. If you are lucky, your dog will readily accept any form of medicine, either straight from your hand or mixed with its food. However, if your dog does not take medicine willingly, you must administer it in some other way.

Powdered medications can be mixed with water and, like liquid medications, drawn into a syringe without a needle in it. Open the lips on the side of your dog's mouth near its molars. While loosely holding the dog's muzzle shut, let the liquid flow slowly into the space between the molars, allowing your dog time to swallow, until all of the liquid is taken. Never squirt the liquid into the mouth. This can cause coughing, resistance, and needless anxiety.

If your dog objects to taking a pill or capsule, first try concealing it inside some hamburger meat or a piece of cheese. If you cannot get your pet to swallow the medication through deception, you may have to use force. Hold the dog's upper jaw and, exerting mild pressure, raise its head. This should cause the dog's mouth to open. Quickly place the pill or capsule on the back of its tongue, hold its mouth closed, tilt its head upward, and rub

its throat in a downward direction. This procedure will force your dog to swallow the pill or capsule.

You will almost certainly need help if you must administer a suppository. Be sure to wear a disposable glove for hygienic reasons. Have your assistant hold the dog with an arm across its chest, and insert the suppository as far into the anus as possible.

When It's Time to Say Good-bye

The most difficult time you may have to face as a pet owner occurs when your loving and loyal friend becomes terminally ill and will soon die. While modern veterinary medicine has many ways to extend your pet's life, you must be aware that no dog will live forever. You should realize also that in some cases veterinary care can serve no useful purpose. If your dog is terminally ill and is experiencing severe and constant pain, aggressive medical attention will not extend life but rather will only prolong the dying process.

Euthanasia is the act by which a veterinarian painlessly induces death, ending the suffering of a terminally ill animal. When you must make the painful decision to have your dog put to sleep, consider the animal's feelings as well as your own. This is never an easy choice. Nevertheless, it has been made in the past by millions of pet owners who loved their friends and companions as much as you love yours. A caring veterinarian will understand the choices you may have to make and will be supportive and open to discussion. Keep in mind, however, that no one else can tell you what to do, and the decision must ultimately be made by you alone.

Breeding and Showing Cocker Spaniels

Breeding Objectives

As the owner of a beautiful, loving, well-behaved cocker spaniel, you will no doubt foster the idea of breeding it in hopes of creating progeny just like your pet. Before you decide to act upon these feelings, however, there are several points you should consider.

Breeding dogs is a serious responsibility that should never be taken lightly. There are far too many unwanted dogs in the world, and to help alleviate this unfortunate situation, the breeder must have plans for each and every puppy *before* the litter is conceived.

You should also forget about breeding if you thought that you could profit economically from this endeavor. In fact, some of the best breeders in the world barely recoup their investments when all is said and done. After they have paid stud fees, provided veterinary care and food for the mother and her litter, and accounted for a huge investment of time and energy, usually little or nothing is left that could be called profit. What breeding dogs does offer you is a sense of responsibility and the exciting challenge of building a solid foundation for future generations of cocker spaniels.

The major objective of every dog breeder should be to produce and raise puppies that will uphold the quality of the physical traits and temperament of the breed. Serious breeders seek to improve their dogs by mating them with quality animals from other kennels. Their main goal is to develop a bloodline of their own that reflects the characteristics outlined in the breed standard.

The Cocker Spaniel Standard (described earlier in this book) is a written description of how the perfect cocker should look, act, and move. Of course, no one has ever produced the perfect cocker, and probably no one ever will. It is the breeder's goal, however, to come as close as possible.

If you should decide to become a breeder, it is hoped that you will embrace the belief that each new litter your dogs produce should be an improvement on the last. To do this you will have to choose your female cocker's mates carefully, seeking out those that will strengthen your dog's weaknesses and emphasize her good qualities. You should also keep in mind that the results and rewards of your good work will be long-lived.

Choosing a Mate

There are three important points to keep in mind when selecting a mate for your female cocker. First, be sure to select a male whose strongest qualities will complement your female's weaknesses. For example, if your dog's coat is not as good as it might be, find a mate from a line of dogs with thick coats. Of course, selecting breeding partners is much more complex than this point implies because you have to weigh all the factors, not just one trait, that make up the two animals.

Second, select a dog with the proper temperament. Temperament is a hereditary trait. A cocker should have the calm, steady disposition of a hunting dog, and you should therefore avoid breeding dogs that are shy or fearful. To do so would be a disservice to both the dogs and to the humans who would purchase puppies that might grow to be skittish or bad tempered.

Third, find a mate that is healthy and free of hereditary defects, some of which are potentially crippling or even fatal. It is the primary responsibility of every breeder to make sure that all of his or her dogs are free of the major hereditary diseases known to affect the breed in question. Imagine how you would feel if the beautiful puppies that you placed in loving homes were to develop a crippling hip problem, or an eye disease that could lead to blindness. Please do not take this warning lightly. Both your dog's breeder and your veterinarian can advise you in regard to inherent defects, so ignorance is no excuse for violating this responsibility.

Finding a suitable mate with the proper temperament and state of health can be very difficult.

Breeding and Showing Cocker Spaniels

You will almost certainly have to familiarize yourself with the genetics of dog breeding. There are many good books devoted entirely to this topic, and I urge you to read some of these, as well as to seek the advice of several experienced breeders, before you begin your adventure into dog breeding.

When you finally decide that it is time to seek out a stud dog, you can obtain a list of those available from the American Spaniel Club. As you visit each breeder on your list, study the dogs to be sure that they have all of the qualities you are seeking. Examine each dog's pedigree to be sure that all is in order. The pedigreee will indicate whether there are any champions in the stud dog's bloodlines.

Once you have chosen a mate for your female, you will have to reach an agreement with the male's breeder on the stud fee. Normally, the cost for the services of a champion stud dog will be greater than that for a nonchampion. Sometimes the breeder may demand the pick of the litter, rather than money. Either way, the terms of the arrangement should be agreed upon in advance.

Breeding Your Female

Your female cocker will probably come into her first estrus (be "in heat" or "in season") when she is eight to ten months old. Estrus refers to a period of time during which the female will accept mating. This period usually lasts about a week but may be as long as two weeks. You should wait, however, until the female's second or third "season" before you breed her; it is important that she is mature enough to deal with the physical and mental demands of motherhood. Normally, a female cocker will come into season twice a year, but it is not advisable to breed her every time. If you breed her once a year until she is about six years old, she should have plenty of time to recuperate between pregnancies.

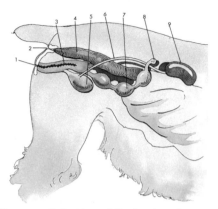

The urogenital system of the female cocker spaniel

1. vulva	4. rectum	7. developing embryo
2. anus	5. bladder	8. ovary
3. vagina	6. ureter	9. kidney

During the seasons when she is not being bred, you must be extremely careful not to let her come near male dogs of any breed. This precaution may not be as easy as it sounds because during estrus the female excretes a scent that attracts male dogs from far and wide. Your female may also have ideas of her own during these periods and, if not kept on a leash, will go off to seek a mate. It is therefore extremely important that you keep your female cocker either confined or restrained on a close leash whenever she is in season, except in the presence of a desired stud dog. You will also have to maintain your vigil even after she has been mated, for male dogs will still be attracted to her until she is definitely out of season.

It is also perfectly natural for a female to discharge blood during estrus. To prevent staining to your rugs or furniture, you may want to confine her to a room that is easily cleaned. Sanitary napkins are also available for dogs in heat.

Before your female experiences the estrus when you plan to breed her, take her to the veterinarian to be checked for worms and to get any booster shots that may be needed. The veterinarian will also be

Breeding and Showing Cocker Spaniels

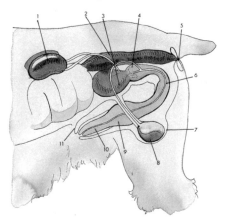

The urogenital system of the male cocker spaniel

1. kidneys	5. anus	9. bulb
2. rectum	6. urethra	10. penis
3. bladder	7. scrotum	11. sheath
4. prostate	8. testes	

The Birth and Care of Puppies

Pregnancy and Birth

The normal cocker pregnancy lasts for about 63 days after conception. You should see the signs of a successful mating after five or six weeks as the female's abdomen swells. Veterinarians, however, can usually diagnose pregnancy through various techniques at four weeks. Once pregnancy is confirmed, it's time to review with your veterinarian the special feeding requirements and your responsibilities before, during, and after the birth.

A few days before your female cocker gives birth (also known as "whelping"), she may refuse to eat and may start to build the nest where she plans to have her puppies. It is therefore important that you introduce her to her whelping box ahead of time; otherwise, she may decide to have the puppies in a closet, under the bed, or in some other inappropriate place.

The whelping box should be sufficiently large to accommodate a stretched-out cocker. It should have low sides and be placed in a private, warm, dry, and draft-free place. You should place towels or other soft material in the bottom of the box. Newspaper is also fine and can easily be replaced as it becomes soiled during the birth. Once whelping is complete, however, you should replace the newspaper with something that provides better footing for the puppies.

Before whelping, your female should begin losing the hair on her undersides to allow the puppies better access to her nipples. If this does not happen, you will have to shave her belly yourself. Shortly before whelping, your female's body temperature will drop from about 101.5°F (38.6°C) to about 99°F (37.1°C). About 24 hours after this drop, your dog can be expected to enter the first stages of labor. She will begin to pant, strain, and appear restless, and may even vomit. Shortly thereafter she will begin the actual birth process.

able to tell if the female is in breeding condition. For breeding, she must be neither over- nor underweight and should show good muscle tone.

When your female's season is near, check her daily for swelling of her vulva, which will become more red in color. As soon as you see the swelling and color, make an appointment with the owner of the stud dog. The best time to breed the female is from 9 to 14 days after the first signs of color; she will be ready for mating when the color changes from dark red to yellow.

In dog breeding, the female is always brought to the male. Once there, little more is required than to introduce your ready and willing female to the experienced stud dog. Once the mating has taken place, allow the coupled dogs to separate on their own; forcing them apart can cause injury. Once separated, put your female back in her cage or in your car, and do not allow her to urinate for a half hour. Now you should prepare both yourself and the cocker for the most wonderful moment of dog breeding, the birth of puppies.

56

Most female cockers give birth easily, without the need of human assistance. Each puppy emerges in its own placental membrane, which the mother will remove so that the puppy can breathe. She does this by tearing the membrane off and eating it; she also severs the umbilical cord with her teeth. After delivery, she will lick each puppy to stimulate breathing.

During the birth process, the new mother will be busy cleaning her offspring, warming them, and allowing them to suckle. It is very important that the puppies suckle soon after emerging from the womb, so that they will receive the antibodies contained in their mother's milk. These will help the puppies fight infection during their early days while their own immune systems are developing.

Occasionally, a new mother may neglect to, or may not be able to, remove the membrane or sever the umbilical cord. In these cases, you will have to perform these tasks yourself and to do so without delay. Remove the puppy from the sac by tearing the membrane first from the face and head and then working backward. Clean any mucus or fluid from the puppy's nose and mouth, and stimulate circulation by rubbing the little creature briskly with a towel. Then pinch the umbilical cord firmly with your fingers or a pair of pliers, cut it about two inches from the abdomen with a pair of scissors, and apply iodine to the cut end to prevent infection.

Needs of the Newborn Puppy

The newborn puppies will be unable to control their own body temperature so they must be kept in a place where the temperature is at least 80°F (27°C). You can also keep the whelping box warm by means of a well-insulated heating pad or an electric heating bulb, but be sure the temperature remains constant and does not become too high.

While newborn cocker puppies are incredibly cute and adorable, you will see immediately that they have very little resemblence to their parents. Do not worry, for they will grow to be more like the adults with each passing day. Perhaps the most

A mother cocker nurses her litter in a whelping box.

obvious difference between your newborns and their mother will be the comparative lengths of their tails. It is general practice to "dock" the long tails of newborn cockers, and this should be done by your veterinarian within 72 hours after the puppies are born. Docking the tails at this age is painless; and if you ever expect your dogs to compete in dog shows, it must be done.

For the first few weeks of their lives the puppies will be totally cared for by their mother. This is especially important when you consider that when cocker puppies are born they cannot see or hear. Besides nursing the puppies, the mother will frequently lick them in order to stimulate them to excrete waste. Without the mother's assistance, puppies cannot excrete. The mother will then also lick up the excretion in order to keep the whelping box clean. In truth, for the first few weeks you will have very little to do besides changing the lining of the box when needed. Enjoy the respite while you can, however, because by the time the puppies are three or four weeks old, they will begin to become more active.

Weaning

By the third or fourth week the puppies' eyes are completely open and their hearing is more acute. They are also becoming much more aware of their surroundings. At this time you will have to begin to wean them, that is, to persuade them to stop depending on their mother for food and to eat on their own. You must begin the weaning process a soon as possible because the mother's milk supply will quickly run short.

Weaning can sometimes be a little difficult, and I have found the following technique to work the best. Purchase a high-quality commercial puppy food, and soften it with hot water until you have a thin, lukewarm mush. Place the food in a shallow plate, and put the puppies around it. Then, dipping your finger into the food, smear some on the end of each puppy's nose. Most puppies will stick out their tiny pink tongues and clean off the end of their button noses. After this procedure has been repeated a few times, the puppies usually begin to sniff at the plate and then eat from it on their own.

As the puppies become more confident and begin to seek out the plate each time it is placed on the floor, you can gradually decrease the amount of water you add to the food. Eventually they will reach the point where they are eating dry food.

Care of the Older Puppy

As the puppies grow older, they will begin to become bolder and will wander about and explore their surroundings. When this phase starts, you will again have to "puppy-proof" your home. At this point you should begin treating the puppies just as you did their mother when you first obtained her.

At the age of about six or seven weeks the puppies should visit the veterinarian to have their booster shots and to be checked for worms. This is also the time when your puppies must leave each other for new homes. Your local cocker spaniel club can help you to find potential buyers for the puppies.

A final note on breeding: Always remember that it is your duty as a responsible breeder to make sure that all of your puppies go to good homes. Don't be afraid to ask prospective buyers about their homes and their views on dog ownership. After all, you have invested a great deal of time, effort, and money into producing the best puppies

Scenes like this one are what breeding is all about. Take note of the variety of expressions among the puppies, and the friendly yet alert mother.

you could, and it would be a great shame if your cockers were sold to persons who could or would not give them the care and the love they need.

Bench Competitions

Any purebred dog, such as a cocker spaniel, which has its pedigree papers and is registered with the AKC, may be entered in any dog show that has suitable judging for that breed. The term "dog show" usually refers to a bench competition in which a dog is judged on its appearance, physique, bearing, and temperament. In these events, a dog is judged strictly on how it conforms to the standard for that breed, as compared to all the other dogs entered in the competition.

At these shows, dogs compete for points that count toward championship status. In the United States, 15 points are required for a dog to become a Champion of Record, entitling the owner to use "CH" before the dog's name. It is possible for dogs to compete in several classes, some of which are restricted by age, sex, and previous wins. The number of points earned usually depends on the number of competitors entered.

Field Trials and Hunting Tests

Cocker spaniels are a breed that is automatically eligible for field trials and hunting tests. Field trials are practical demonstrations of a dog's ability to perform, in an outdoor environment, the functions for which it was bred. The titles awarded are Field Champion and Amateur Field Champion. Cockers may also participate in hunting tests, in which the dogs are judged on their ability to perform during a hunt. The best dogs may be awarded the titles of Junior Hunter, Senior Hunter, and Master Hunter.

Both field trials and hunting tests are sponsored by the AKC. If you wish to have your cocker compete in either or both of these events, you can get a list of rules and the dates of such competitions from the AKC or your local cocker club.

Obedience Trials

Obedience trials test your cocker's ability to perform a prescribed set of commands. There are three different levels in which a dog may compete; Novice, Open, and Utility, with each more difficult than its predecessor.

Novice exercises test all the abilities that should be taught to make a cocker a good companion animal. These include heeling, as well as obedience to "come" and "stay" commands. A successful dog earns the title Champion Dog (CD).

The Open division exercises include retrieving, jumping, hurdles, and broad jumping. A dogs that earns an Open title is called a Companion Dog Excellent (CDX).

To earn the title of Utility Dog (UD), a cocker must learn scent discrimination and hand signals, among other skills. Only dogs awarded the Utility Dog title can earn points toward an Obedience Trial Championship (OTCH), which is the top honor a dog can earn in these trials.

Because obedience trials, bench competitions, field trials, and hunting tests all have different formats and separate sets of rules, you should attend as many of them as possible to observe the judging. These shows also are a great learning experience. Manufacturers of dog food and other pet products often attend and display their merchandise. You will also be able to learn from expert breeders and judges, who can advise the novice on the care and grooming of cocker spaniels.

If you wish to enter your dog in a show, check with your local cocker spaniel club. This organization can advise you about the rules of the event, help you obtain and complete the application forms, and inform you of the entry fee.

A Hunter's Perspective

I recently met an elderly Australian gentleman at a major dog show in the United States. As I stood talking to some of the exhibitors, he approached and asked us why all the cockers he had seen had coats that he considered too long for a hunting breed. When asked why he had inquired, the gentleman proceeded to tell us of all the hunting dogs he had owned over the years. His favorites were a pair of black cockers with which he would go birding. These cockers, he claimed, were about the same size as the dogs in the ring that day, but he insisted (and rather strongly, I might add) that the coats of the show dogs were much too long to be practical for hunting dogs. When we told him that the judges seemed to prefer this length, he started to walk away, shaking his head and muttering. As I stood there pondering the conversation, he turned and told me (with what I believed to be a tear in his eye) that he was afraid that cockers had finally gone the way of poodles and afghans. With that, he walked off, never to be seen—at least by me—again.

For those who may not know, it should be explained that both poodles and afghans were originally bred as hunting dogs. Dogs of these breeds that are shown in the ring today, however, have little resemblance to their hunting ancestors—the point, I guess, that the gentleman was trying to bring to our attention. And, indeed, it is true that the cockers shown in bench competition today are more stylized and cosmetically enhanced than were their forebearers of, say, 40 or 50 years ago.

While I cannot say whether this change is for better or worse, I am confident that the appearance of cockers in the show ring will not change much unless or until the judges begin to interpret the AKC Standard differently. Cockers entered in obedience or field competitions, however, are not judged on their looks. As a result, most of the cockers participating in these competitions do indeed have coats of shorter length than their relatives appearing in bench competitions. For the cocker required to jump obstacles or retrieve downed fowl from a pond, a shorter, less cumbersome coat is much more practical.

The moral of this story is that no individual dog can please everybody. Although it would be great if your cocker happened to delight each ring judge who saw it, you should really not count on such a happening, for dogs of this caliber are extremely rare. What is much more important is that your dog pleases you. You should never blame your dog for failure in the ring, for if the judging were up to your cocker, it would win every award possible to please you.

Therefore, go to the shows, have a good time, and learn all you can. Afterward, bring your beloved pet back home and show it that you still believe it to be the best cocker spaniel in the world.

Basic and Advanced Training

Setting Up a Good Program

Like most hunting dogs, the cocker spaniel is relatively easy to train. Because of several hundred years of close hunter-dog relationships, the cocker has an innate willingness to learn. For this reason you can begin to train your cocker at an earlier age than is possible with many other breeds. Likewise, the cocker's acquired hunting-dog attentiveness will permit longer training sessions, thus leading to quicker learning. While it is possible to teach your cocker just about anything, this chapter deals primarily with the basic lessons that every dog should know, as well as some of the fundamental exercises for the prospective gundog.

Bear in mind that, while every cocker has the ability to learn and perform these exercises it is up to you, its master, to teach the lessons properly. This instruction will take time, energy, and patience. Your puppy will depend on you to find the right method to teach it. Once this method is established, however, your cocker will respond both eagerly and joyfully.

The ten rules listed below will help you to set up a good training program for your puppy. It is important that these rules be established before you begin training and be adhered to closely at each session. If you do this, you will be giving your cocker the best chance to learn its lessons as thoroughly and rapidly as possible.

1. Begin working with your puppy the day you bring it home. Hold two or three sessions a day, and continue these sessions as long as your puppy shows interest. By limiting the sessons to 10 or 15 minutes each, you will provide sufficient teaching without boring your dog. Your puppy may need two weeks or longer to begin to understand some of your commands, so do not neglect your training. Cockers must learn these basic lessons at a very early age.

2. Be consistent. All the members of your household must decide what is permitted and what is not. Once you have taught your dog a lesson, never allow it to do the contrary without reprimand.

3. Be authoritative. Deliver all visual and verbal commands clearly and unmistakably. Because dogs understand tones better than words, be sure your reprimands are always sharp and firm, while your praise is calm and friendly. Although your dog must learn that you are in charge, *never* demonstrate authority by using physical force. Besides being totally unnecessary, forcing a dog to perform or hitting it only teaches it to dislike training sessions.

4. Conduct each training session in an atmosphere conducive to learning. Have your dog learn the lesson with as few distractions as possible. In adddition, never attempt to teach a puppy anything if you are in a bad mood. Your negative attitude will only confuse the puppy and make learning harder.

5. Do not attempt to teach your dog more than one concept in a single training session, and never move on to another concept until your pet has mastered the previous one. Puppies, like people, learn at their own pace and should never be rushed.

6. Praise your dog generously after it has performed correctly. Verbal praise and petting or scratching behind the ears will make your cocker an eager student. Although it is commonplace for trainers to reward their pupils with food, this practice is not neccessary. Your puppy should learn to perform correctly with the incentive of your enthusiastic praise.

7. Punish disobedience immediately. Because a puppy has a very short memory, never put off a reprimand. If, for example, your puppy chews your slipper, do not punish it unless you catch it in the act; otherwise, it will not understand why you are displeased. An adult dog that knows better, however, can be reprimanded for the same offense after showing it the slipper.

8. Generally limit punishment to verbal reprimands. In extreme conditions you may place the dog in its cage after reprimanding it.
9. Even when your dog is older, keep your training sessions short and end them early if the dog begins to lose interest.
10. Never try to teach your dog a lesson when it is tired; a tired dog is much less likely to learn readily and properly. If you hold your training sessions before you feed your dog, it is less likely to be sleepy and sluggish.

Cockers are a unique and entertaining breed to train because, while they are rapid and attentive learners, they are also opportunists and will try to take advantage of every break they are given. For instance, if you are not firm enough in your commands, your dog may pretend that it did not hear you and go on with whatever activity it chooses. If you should then get upset and yell, it will find a way to punish you for injuring its pride. One of my cockers, before obeying my commands, would run around or under every jumping hurdle until she finally got me to smile and laugh. Once that was done, she began to perform as expected.

I have found from experience that cockers can be trained much more easily by using smiles and encouragement rather than anger and physical force. Therefore, if you are in the middle of a training session and your student's attention starts to wander, or if you feel you are being ignored, consider ending the lesson early and reviewing the rules of training. When you find out what the problem was, be sure to correct it in your next session.

Training a Puppy

Presumably, you will have chosen a name for your puppy before picking it up. Therefore, the first lesson, teaching your puppy its name, will actually begin the moment you leave the breeder's house. This is one of the easiest lessons to teach,

You should start training your puppy as soon as possible. Be sure you have its total attention, and use hand gestures to help the puppy understand your verbal commands.

for all you do is address your puppy by name each time you talk to it. You will be amazed at how fast the puppy will learn this lesson. Just be sure to use the same name all the time and to avoid the urge to use nicknames, which will only lead to confusion.

The next important lesson to teach your cocker puppy is the word "no." There is little doubt that you will have ample opportunity to teach this lesson in the first few days the puppy is in your home. Whenever you see it do something wrong, say "No" in a sharp, firm tone that shows you are serious. If the puppy refuses to listen, pick it up and place it in its cage. Remember never to use force, which will only make the puppy hand-shy.

Cockers come in a variety of colors, including (clockwise, from top left) solid black, solid dark tan, white and tan, and black and white.

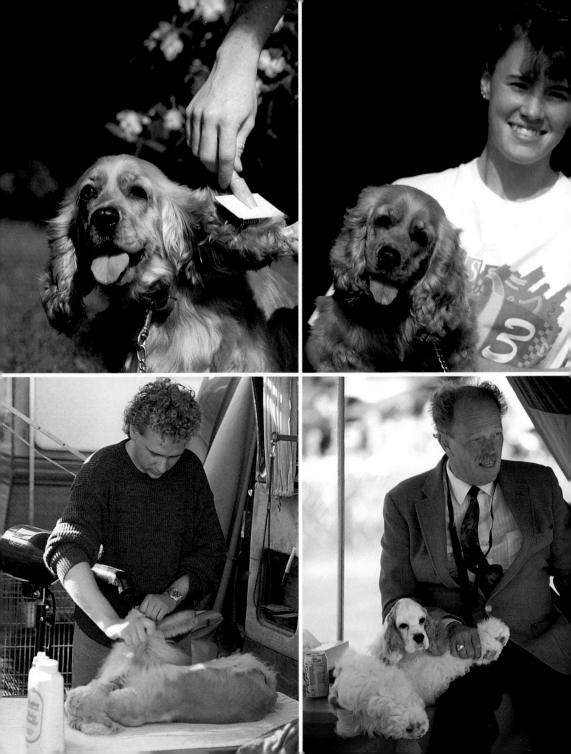

Basic and Advanced Training

Using a cage will simplify training in general and can be a tremendous aid in housebreaking a puppy.

Housebreaking

For obvious reasons, housebreaking a puppy has never been a lot of fun for the dog owner. There are certain methods, however, that can speed up the process and avoid a lot of the surprises associated with it.

Outdoor Training: Outdoor training begins when you first bring your puppy home. Before taking it indoors, walk it to the area you have chosen for it to eliminate. Give your cocker plenty of time to relieve itself, and praise it thoroughly when it is done. Verbal praise and petting will reinforce your puppy's confidence and will increase the chances of a successful repeat performance later on.

Since most puppies have to relieve themselves as many as six times a day, you should take your pet outdoors about once every three or four hours. It is also advisable to walk the puppy after every one of its meals. When a puppy's stomach is full, extra pressure is exerted on the bladder, so it is best not to wait too long. You should take your puppy for its last walk as late in the evening as possible, thereby increasing your cocker's chances of making it through the night without accidents. If you continue to bring your puppy to the same area each time and to praise it for each successful performance, it will eventually seek out this area on its own.

All cockers require and benefit from frequent grooming (top), but cockers that are exhibited in bench competitions require an especially thorough grooming prior to the show (bottom left). Once groomed, these beautiful dogs eagerly wait with their handlers until it is their turn to perform (bottom right).

Indoor Techniques: There are two different methods you can use for indoor housebreaking. One method involves paper; the other, the use of a cage. The objective of paper training is to get your puppy to urinate and defecate on newspapers spread out in an area of your choosing. Kitchens and bathrooms make the best locations because they are easy to clean. The papers, however, must not be placed too close to the puppy's eating or sleeping areas, since your cocker will make every effort to keep those areas clean and will not excrete near them.

At first you can confine your puppy to the room you have chosen until it voids. If it uses the paper, remove the top sheets and place fresh, clean papers under what were formerly the bottom sheets. By doing this, you will be leaving the scent from the bottom papers exposed so that the puppy can relocate the area more easily to repeat the act.

If the puppy misses the paper at first, attempt to get the scent of the dog's urine onto a sheet of newspaper and place it on top of the other sheets. Then thoroughly clean the inappropriate area that the puppy used. It is important that the puppy seek out its scent on the papers and not find it on the floor, where it will repeat its action.

Cage training offers an easier and faster alternative to paper training and takes advantage of the fact that your puppy will instinctively try to keep its sleeping area clean. If your puppy is wary on its first encounter with the cage, make the cage more appealing by placing some toys inside for your pet to play with. After you have confined the puppy to its cage a few times with its excreta, it will quickly learn to restrain itself until you let it out of the cage. Of course, after you release the puppy from its cage, you must take it outdoors immediately. Establish a time schedule for it to relieve itself before bringing it back indoors. As your trust in your puppy grows, you can let it out for longer and longer periods until eventually you can leave the cage door open at all times without fear of "accidents," provided that you take the dog outside as scheduled.

Basic and Advanced Training

Using a cage also has additional benefits. Before domestication, dogs were cave-dwelling animals. Instinctively, the modern dog finds security in any cavelike structure once it becomes familiar with it. If you choose to use a cage, you will find that your dog will actually prefer to sleep there and will return on its own. In addition to its use in housebreaking, a cage, therefore, can serve as a sleeping box and a traveling crate and can also prove helpful when you are unable to supervise the puppy.

No matter which method of housebreaking you choose for your puppy, it is inevitable that "accidents" will eventually occur. If you discover that while you slept your puppy could no longer control itself, it will do no good to administer punishment. Puppies have very short memories, so if you do not catch your puppy in the act, or make the discovery shortly afterward, a scolding will only confuse your pet. Should you catch your cocker in the act, rebuke it with a sharp "No!" and then put it in its cage. Never spank your puppy, and never put the puppy's nose in the mess. Not only is this an unsanitary thing to do, but also it may well upset the puppy to the point that you will have one more thing to clean up.

Walking on a Leash

This is another lesson that should begin as soon as you bring your puppy home. Each time you take your cocker out to relieve itself or to exercise it, you should put on its collar (making sure it is neither too tight nor too loose) and attach a leash of sufficient length. As you walk, hold the leash on your left side and use gentle persuasion to keep the puppy close to your leg. Do not allow the puppy to get under your feet or to run ahead of you. Remain patient. A cocker puppy's legs are very short, and it is not capable of tremendous speed. If your puppy falls behind, do not attempt to drag it forward. Use friendly words, patience, and, if necessary, a tiny bit of gentle physical persuasion to keep your puppy in its proper walking position.

Obedience Training

Obedience training is extremely important, and the basic exercises should be learned by every dog. Even if you decide not to enter your dog in an obedience trial, these lessons will help you to handle your dog properly in awkward situations and may even help save your pet from harm. All of the lessons in this group can be taught to your dog at home. However, if you prefer to seek the services of an expert dog handler, you can sign your cocker up for obedience classes.

Obedience schools provide the proper atmosphere for teaching your dog all it must learn to compete in shows, as well as how it should act in the world of humans, and offer an interesting and easy alternative to training your dog yourself. You may wish to have an older child in your household take the dog to these classes. In this way the child and the dog can spend more time together and the child learns the responsibilities of proper pet care.

A list of reputable obedience schools in your area can be obtained from your local cocker club or the AKC. Before enrolling your dog, however, make sure that the class suits your purpose. Some schools have special classes for show-dog handling as well as sessions designed for amateurs.

Basic Commands

The first three commands to teach your puppy are Sit, Stay, and Come. To make it easy for your cocker to recognize these commands, you should keep them short and simple: for example, "Sit" or "Sit, Millie" instead of "Sit over there, Millie." While dogs are fairly smart, they do not understand complete sentences. Instead they rely on hearing the command word and interpreting your tone of voice and body gestures.

Sit: Take your puppy into an isolated room, and fit it with a collar and leash. Holding the leash with your right hand, place your left hand on the puppy's hindquarters. Then give the command

Basic and Advanced Training

Eye contact is important in teaching each training exercise. It helps your dog to interpret your wishes and to keep its attention on the business at hand.

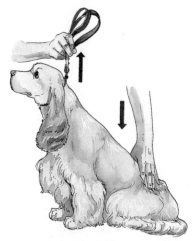

In teaching the "Sit" command, use one hand to gently push the hindquarters down, and the other hand to keep the dog's head upright with the aid of a leash.

"Sit!" or "Sit, Millie!" in a firm voice, at the same time pressing gently and steadily on the dog's hindquarters. Gently pull the leash upward to keep your puppy from lying down on the floor. Hold the dog in this position for a while; do not allow it to jump back up.

Repeat the procedure until the session ends or until the puppy begins to lose interest. Remember to praise your cocker each time it sits properly, but do not expect it to master this command perfectly in the first training session.

Once your puppy has performed the Sit at least a couple of times in succession, remove the leash and give the command. If your dog does not perform correctly, remain patient and try again with the leash on. Repetition and consistency are the keys to teaching this lesson. With proper training it should not take very long for your cocker to master this command.

If you plan on entering your cocker in field trials or are considering using it as a hunting dog, you should teach it to respond to hand signals and whistles as well as the spoken word. In the field, your cocker may be at a distance where it cannot clearly hear your commands, but can see gestures or hear the sharp, piercing sound of a whistle. Thus, even at a distance you can still have some control over your dog. Once your dog has mastered the command, hold up either your entire hand or a single finger in a distinct gesture and say "Sit," making sure the dog can see the signal. Always use the word (or sound) and the gesture together so that your dog connects the two.

Stay: This command is usually more difficult to teach because your puppy will always want to be at your side, and "Stay" orders your dog to remain wherever it is. However, this command may someday save your dog's life, should it start to run into a busy street.

In teaching your dog the Stay, first fit it with a leash and collar. Then run through the Sit procedure, and follow it with the command "Stay." As you say this new command, raise your hand, palm toward the dog, like a police officer stopping traffic. Each time your dog attempts to stand up, reproach it with a sharp "No!"

Basic and Advanced Training

Use the proper hand signal when teaching. In this case the cocker will associate a flat, open-handed gesture with the "Stay" command.

Take up all the slack in the leash to hold your student in place, and repeat the procedure until the dog appears to understand. Then remove the leash and repeat the command several times. Praise the dog each time it obeys, and reprimand disobedience.

Continue this command until your cocker has repeated the act with consistent success. Then slowly back away from the dog, making sure to maintain eye contact. As you move backward, keep repeating "Stay." If your cocker attempts to follow, utter a loud, sharp "No!" If the dog continues forward, reprimand it. Naturally a dog that stays when told deserves lavish praise.

Come: Although for the most part your puppy will race to you when you call its name, the trick to the Come command is to have your cocker come to you obediently when something of greater interest is attracting its attention. You should teach the command "Come" to your puppy right after "Sit" and "Stay." Start by running through the procedures for these two commands. Once your puppy has stayed at a good distance, call the dog by name (for example, "Millie") and follow with the command "Millie, Come." Accompany your words with a lively sound or gesture, such as clapping your hands or slapping your thighs, to help excite your dog into motion.

Your little student will quickly associate the word "Come" with your movements. Praise it for responding correctly. If it does not respond to the command, put the puppy on a long rope and let it wander off. Then slowly reel in the rope while repeating the word "Come!" Shower your dog with praise when it reaches you. Repeat this exercise several times; then try it without the rope again. While using a rope may seem drastic, it is important that your cocker master this exercise, for, like "Stay," the "Come" command can help protect your dog from accidents.

Heeling

Heeling is a mandatory skill for cockers entered in obedience trials. When your dog heels properly, it will walk on your left with its head about the same distance forward as your knees. When you begin teaching your dog this lesson, you will require a leash. Eventually, though, your cocker must learn to heel without the restraint of the leash.

To start, run through all the other commands your dog has mastered. Successful performance will give your dog extra confidence before you start this difficult lesson. Hold the end of the leash in your right hand, and grab about halfway toward the collar with your left hand. Begin a brisk walk, giving the sharp command "Heel!" and using your left hand to control and guide.

If your dog lags behind, pull gently on the leash to bring it even with your leg. Do not drag the dog forward or force it to obey your commands, lest you destroy the well-established learning atmosphere. If your dog runs forward, pull it back to your side and give the "Heel" command again.

If you have difficulty getting your dog to perform correctly, run through the Sit and Stay exercises. Once again, praise successes and repri-

Basic and Advanced Training

For the proper heeling position, always keep the dog on your left side. For better control, "choke up" on the leash.

mand disobedience. When the Sit and the Stay have been performed correctly, begin the Heel exercises again.

The Heel lesson is very difficult for a dog to learn, so take your time and be patient. Once the command "Heel" on a leash, has been mastered, take your student through a turning exercise. If it has trouble heeling while you turn, take a shorter grip on the leash, and bring the dog closer to your side. Then repeat the command "Heel!" in a sharp tone, and gently persuade your puppy to follow you by lightly pulling on the leash. As your cocker gains confidence, take it through a series of straight line, right turn, and left turn exercises.

Once your pet has mastered turning, it is time to begin training with a slack leash. Go through the Heel exercise with the leash exerting no pressure on your dog's collar. At the first mistake, grasp the leash firmly and lead the dog steadily in the proper direction. When it performs correctly, praise it generously.

When your dog has learned to walk correctly with a slack leash, remove the leash completely. If your puppy has performed with a loose leash, you should be able to achieve the same results without a leash, provided that you do not change your routine. Continue to praise or reprimand as warranted. If you have trouble, you will have to put the leash back on and repeat the lesson.

Keep in mind that the Heel is very difficult to master. If you are patient and persistent, however, your dog will eventually learn its lesson.

Lying Down

Have your cocker assume a sitting position, and then slowly pull its front legs forward while saying "Down!" If your dog attempts to stand up, give it a sharp "No!" If necessary, push down on the dog's shoulders at the same time that you pull its front legs slowly forward. While you do this, give the command "Down!" Because you will have both hands occupied, you should carefully step on the leash to prevent the dog from returning to its feet. Keep the dog in the lying position for about one minute, and gradually increase this time period as your dog progresses.

When your pupil has mastered this lesson, begin to move away, while maintaining constant eye contact. Whenever the dog attempts to stand up, repeat the command "Down!" in a firm, sharp tone. Continue the lessons until you are satisfied with the results, and remember to praise your puppy for each successful performance.

Extra Training for Hunting Dogs

While the skills described in this section are all required in the obedience ring, they are also desirable for a hunting dog. These exercises can be difficult for a cocker to master, so be patient and understanding.

Relinquishing an Object

Every dog must be taught to give up any object, no matter how desirable, on command. For hunting dogs it is doubly important that they relinquish their prey as soon as their master tells them to do so. For training purposes, you can substitute a piece of nonsplintering wood for a downed woodcock.

Give your cocker the wood to hold in its teeth. Then command your dog to sit, praising it when it obeys. Using both hands, slowly pull the dog's jaws apart, while saying, "Let go!" in a strict, firm tone. If your dog begins to growl, give it a sharp "No!" Do not be afraid if your cocker growls. This is a dog's way of trying to establish its dominance, and a natural reaction to anyone who attempts to seize its prey. You must, however, make it clear to your dog that you are the boss by taking the object away. Once your dog accepts you as a dominant force, it will give up the wood without any objection.

Retrieving

Retrieving is a skill that can be taught fairly easily to most cockers. In fact, a properly trained hunting cocker must flush the game, drop into a sitting position so as not to interfere with the shot, and retrieve on command only. This procedure also includes retrieval from water.

Start by throwing a suitably sized, nonedible ball or stick, with your dog standing next to you, and call out, "Fetch!" If the dog picks up the object in its mouth and returns to you, command your pet to sit, put your hand, palm up, under its jaw, and say, "Let go!" You should be able to remove the object from the dog's mouth without any resistance. If your dog drops the object, place it back in its mouth, and then remove it, saying "Let go!"

If your cocker fails to return with the object, repeat the exercise using a 30-foot (9-m) rope. Tie the dog to the rope, throw the object, and call out, "Fetch!" again. Once the cocker has picked up the object, draw the dog toward you and then take the object from it.

If your dog hesitates to pick up the object, place the object in its mouth and follow the commands in

the preceding section for relinquishing an object. Keep repeating this lesson until the dog understands that this object is to be taken into its mouth. Then throw the object a short distance to see whether the dog will pick it up.

Jumping over Hurdles

Jumping over hurdles is sometimes difficult for a cocker to master. However, a hunting dog must learn to leap over obstacles that separate it from downed prey. First, command your dog to sit on one side of a small pile of boards of reasonable height, while you stand on the opposite side. Then command the dog by saying "Jump!" If it walks around the obstacle, say, "No!" and then bring it back and start over. Be sure to praise your dog for a successful performance.

As your dog learns to jump over the hurdle on command, gradually increase the obstacle's height. Be careful, however, not to make the jump too high, lest your young dog be injured and discouraged from further jumping.

Once your dog has learned to jump on command, begin a jump and retrieve exercise. Place the object to be retrieved on the other side of the hurdle, and command your dog to sit next to you. Then command it to retrieve the object by saying, "Jump! Fetch!" in a clear, firm voice. The dog should leap over the obstacle, pick up the object, and jump back with it. Tell the dog to sit again, and take the object out of its mouth while saying, "Let go!" Finally, praise your dog warmly for its accomplishment.

Tips for Training Older Dogs

As I mentioned earlier, the purpose of training dogs when they are young is to teach them how they are expected to behave before any bad habits can form. For the most part, training an older dog consists primarily of breaking any bad habits it may have picked up that prevent it from accomplishing your goals. These habits may have resulted from failure to observe any one of the rules of training and, once established as part of the dog's behavior, may require drastic action to eliminate.

The first step is to analyze the situation in order to find out, if possible, how the bad habit was formed. For example, a dog that barks excessively may, as a puppy, have been given a reward of food each time it performed the Speak command correctly. As a result, the dog may bark whenever it is hungry or wants a treat. Thus, the best way to correct this behavior is to make sure that the dog is *never* rewarded with food when it barks on command. This method, termed "extinction," calls on the trainer to repeat the Speak command over and over, but never, ever to give a reward except verbal praise and petting.

Bad habits can also be broken by using punishment. The punishment, however, should never include hitting or throwing things at the dog. Instead, each time your dog performs the undesirable conditioned act, it should be scolded with a sharp "No!" If the problem persists, the punishment should be confinement to the cage. Once again, the key to success is to scold or confine the dog every time it exhibits the bad habit. This method works particularly well for breaking nasty habits such as begging or excessive barking and can also be used to control an overaggressive dog.

Solving Problems Encountered in Training

While it is true that no two dogs are alike, and that the ability to learn may vary greatly, every cocker spaniel can master all of the commands and exercises discussed in this chapter. Should your cocker turn out to be a slow learner, be patient, persistent, and understanding. If you display these qualities in your teaching, eventually your dog's training will become complete.

If your dog shows an unwillingness to learn, or seems to be having trouble with a particular lesson, examine your teaching methods. Review the section entitled "Setting Up a Good Program," and go over each of the basic rules of training. Ask yourself whether you have followed these precepts during all of your sessions. Once you have identified the problem, you should correct it immediately.

If, however, after thoroughly reviewing your methods, you feel that your instruction is not the problem, carefully consider your dog and its environment. Could your cocker possibly be distracted by an outside factor? If so, remove the distraction. Could your dog be ill? If an ailment is suspected, make an appointment with your veterinarian.

Finally, should you continue to run into training difficulties, I strongly recommend that you contact a reputable obedience school. In many instances, ego will not allow us to believe that we could be doing anything wrong. The professional dog handlers who run obedience facilities, on the other hand, can usually diagnose and correct problems rather easily.

If you start early and work hard, be assured that your cocker can be trained to whatever stage you desire. Always keep in mind that you will reap the fruits of your labor once the training is complete, for then you will enjoy the companionship of a faithful pet that eagerly waits upon every word and action of its beloved master.

Understanding Cocker Spaniels

The Nature of the Cocker Spaniel

The cocker spaniel is an extremely complex creature. To understand its behavior patterns, we must take a close look at the process by which dogs evolved, became domesticated, and were selectively bred to create the purebreed we know today.

Regardless of breed, all dogs can trace their ancestry to a form of wild dog or wolf. Wolves and wild dogs live in a highly structured society in which members must behave in certain ways so that the pack can function as a group and live in harmony. One of these behavior patterns is called "ranking order."

Ranking order is a process by which the stronger and more experienced animals are placed at the top of the social ladder, whereas the younger and weaker ones are subordinate. In the pack, all dogs submit to one of higher authority. This system, in essence, prevents violent fights from occurring and helps the animals to hunt and coexist as a group, thereby ensuring survival of the species.

The behavior pattern of ranking order is actually instinctive and can be seen in all of our modern dogs. It is the fact that dogs still possess this trait which allows us to train them. During the training process, you, the master, are enforcing your dominance over your pet. Once your puppy understands its subordinate role, it will naturally attempt to follow your commands.

Another instinctive behavior that our modern cocker has inherited is "scent marking." While this trait is more important to males, it plays a role in any dog's life. As you walk your cocker, it will attempt to mark several prominent spots, such as trees, fence posts, and telephone poles, with its urine to designate its territory. Likewise, your dog will use its nose to interpret other scent marks as made by friends or foes.

There are several other instinctive behaviors that cocker spaniels have inherited from their wild ancestors, including their sexual drives and a parent's inborn vigilance to protect its offspring. Like the wild wolves, a female cocker in heat will excrete a strong scent to attract males, and after the birth of her pups will keep them close and shield them from anything she considers dangerous.

All of these inherited behavior patterns have a common denominator: each plays an important role in the survival of the individual and the survival of the species. Survival is of paramount importance to wild dogs and is so strong an instinct that it has never been bred out of any of our modern breeds.

The Effects of Domestication

While instinctive behaviors still play major roles in the lives of modern cockers, as a result of domestication, this breed has developed many new traits that are passed from one generation to the next. All of these qualities resulted from extensive contact with humans.

Once fearful of their two-legged competitors, some wild dogs eventually overcame their apprehension and developed a trust in people. With this came self-confidence. Also, through prolonged contact with humans, dogs were exposed to new experiences and learned new things. Specifically, through their history, the domesticated ancestors of the cocker were exposed to the new experience of hunting with humans.

As one would expect, hunting dogs must undergo extensive training, and thereby encounter a great deal of contact with their owners. After generations of this close relationship with humans, the cocker has become a wonderful companion as well as a hunting aid. The merry, loyal, and obedient nature of the cocker, as well as its physical characteristics, is the result of the careful, selective breeding practices of hunters and other enthusiasts. These breeders have likewise been responsible for weeding out many of the inherent canine behaviors that would be undesirable in a hunting dog.

In summary, the nature of the cocker spaniel is a blend of two separate elements. The first includes all of the inherited behaviors that are the result of the strong survival instincts of the cocker's wild ancestors. The second element consists of the selectively bred traits and characteristics that have evolved in this breed since the time when dogs were first domesticated. It is the combination of the inborn behavior patterns and the character traits acquired over long periods of time that has made the cocker spaniel a loyal hunting companion and one of the most popular dogs in the world.

How Dogs Communicate

In the preceding chapter we pointed out that dog trainers must use vocal tones and body gestures to get their ideas across to their students. It is just as important, however, for pet owners to be able to understand what their dogs are trying to tell them. Cockers will use their voices, body language, and facial expressions to convey their moods and emotions.

While the cocker's primary form of vocal communication is barking, these dogs, like most other breeds, are capable of a variety of sounds, varying from a high-pitched whine to a deep growl. Since dogs rarely make noises without a reason, each individual sound or combination of sounds a cocker makes has a specific purpose. A dog may yelp in fright or pain, whine and whimper when lonely or seeking attention, groan when content or ailing, and bark in anger or glee. If you listen carefully and observe your dog's movements, you will soon learn the meanings of the various sounds.

Body language is an equally important indicator of your dog's mood. A joyous cocker jumps up and down eagerly and may bark, or may roll over exposing its undersides in the hope of a good belly scratching. A dog that crouches and lowers its head to the floor is exhibiting fear, either of punishment, or of an intruder, or of another dog.

The best indicator of your dog's emotions, however, is its tail. A happy dog will wag its tail briskly. It is even possible to tell *how* happy your pet is by how much it wags its tail: the more wag, the happier the dog. Strangely enough, cockers seem to know that their docked tails may not be adequate to tell the whole story, so they tend to wiggle their entire backsides to show how happy they are.

The tail is used to show other emotions as well. A frightened cocker will point its tail straight down. An alert or attentive cocker will raise its tail and hold it perfectly still, while a placidly content dog will hold its tail at a slightly lower angle and wag it slowly.

The contented spaniel may also choose to lie down in a sprawled-out manner, either on its side or on its belly with its head propped up on its paws. A cocker will usually choose to take up this position in a location where it can keep an eye on its beloved master.

When the cocker stretches itself out and tenses its body, this action can mean several things. If the dog's neck hair also stands on end, consider this action a warning of potential danger or anger. Sometimes this position is taken before a defensive stand or an attack. Should a sprawled-out, tense cocker show a wagging or rotating tail, however, the dog is most likely in a joyous or playful mood. This is the type of position a cocker may take before making a mock hunting spring toward its favorite toy.

The final indicator of your cocker's moods are its facial expressions and gestures. This breed uses its eyes, ears, mouth, lips, and tongue to show a variety of feelings from happiness to sadness, joy to anger, cockiness to disappointment, and alertness to mischievousness.

An alert or inquisitive dog will raise the upper portions of its ears, and an inquisitive dog may cock its head to one side and watch you with wide-open eyes. In a contented dog, the mouth is closed and the ears are in normal position. Cockers are capable of expressing many different emotions and will even smile when they are happy. A cocker does this by opening its mouth slightly, sticking out the tip of its tongue, and pulling back on the corners of its lips to expose a portion of its teeth.

Cockers use their mouths and tongues for other purposes as well. A tired or hot dog will open its mouth wide, hang out its tongue, and pant in order to expel excess body heat. The cocker will use its tongue to lick members of its human family in an effort to express its love and devotion. While some people find "dog kisses" a little distasteful, you should never forget that this is how dogs show their closeness with members of their own kind.

A final note on canine communication: Be wary of any dog that has its ears back, its upper lips raised, its mouth open, and the hairs on the back of its neck raised, and that is growling. Although you will rarely see a cocker in this condition, remember that these are all warning signs of fear and/or anger, and that they may presage an attack.

The Cocker's Sense Organs

Dogs in general, and hunting dogs in particular, rely more on their senses of smell and hearing than they do on their other senses.

Your cocker's olfactory system, which governs its sense of smell, is more than 40 times as large as a human's, and it uses this system to a greater extent. A cocker depends on its sense of smell to locate food, find a mate, interpret territorial boundaries, and track down prey during the hunt. Cockers can remember thousands of odors and have the ability to associate them with the proper people, places, and animals.

A cocker's sense of hearing, its auditory system, is also superior to that of humans. Cocker's can hear a wider range of sounds, including very high-pitched frequencies such as those emitted by "silent" dog whistles (Galton whistles). Cockers can also hear sounds at a greater distance than can

humans. Like their keen sense of smell, their acute hearing is important to their skill as hunting dogs, both for locating prey and for taking long distance directions from their masters.

Cockers, like other breeds, also have the ability to differentiate and remember certain sounds. A friend tells me that she knows a few minutes in advance when her husband is coming home, for their cocker becomes all excited at the impending arrival. The dog, it seems, is able to recognize the sound of the family car while it is quite a few blocks away.

Although a cocker's peripheral vision is greater than that of humans, these dogs cannot focus on an object as sharply. As a result, their eyes may not perceive an animal until it starts to move. The hunting cocker, therefore, relies much more on smelling and hearing its prey than on spotting a still target.

While the cocker spaniel's coat offers the dog protection from the elements as well as from thorns and thickets, it also results in a lack of body sensitivity. The body parts not covered by the dense coat, such as the nose and muzzle, however, have a much greater degree of feeling.

Like other dogs, the cocker may also possess other senses that we do not completely understand. Included in these is an innate sense of navigation. We have all heard stories of dogs, lost on vacations, that traveled hundreds of miles to return home. At the present time this phenomenon is being examined by researchers, but there is still no explanation.

In keeping with your cocker's heritage as a hunting dog, it is important that your pet learn not to fear people or other animals with which it comes in contact. Although it is normal for your cocker to be wary of strangers, the dog should never display fear. To help your cocker learn how it should react, you need to introduce it to the outside world and the ways of humans while it is still very young. In addition to eliminating fear, this exposure will help to instill the self-confidence that should be present in all cockers.

Understanding Cocker Spaniels

The following sections are designed to help you understand how your cocker should react to different people and situations and what steps you can take to avoid trouble.

The Cocker and Children

The cocker spaniel has always been hailed as a great lover of home and family, and under normal circumstances is completely trustworthy. This breed has been known to bond closely with children and at times may become extremely protective of them.

A cocker will provide companionship, fun, and enjoyment for all children. A puppy that grows up with them considers itself one of the family. Your cocker will teach your children the importance of affection and warmth, and serve as an example of absolute integrity, for it will never betray them. Cockers are the ultimate playmates because they love to run and frolic, especially with children.

It is important to remember, however, that the cocker, although a very rugged and sturdy dog, is not a physical match for older, boisterous children. While a cocker will normally not object to a little roughhouse play, it may take exception to having its ears, tail, or nose pinched, pushed, or pulled. Therefore, children must be taught how to treat their dog and must be careful to avoid all sensitive areas, especially the eyes. If you have a puppy, you should supervise all play sessions with the children until the dog is both large enough and strong enough for occasional rough handling.

Children should also be taught never to disturb a dog while it is eating or sleeping. Explain to them that, although their dog is a loving pet, it may nip if it is surprised or frightened.

You can ensure a lasting relationship between your cocker and your children by involving them in the responsibilities of dog care. Encourage them to participate in feeding, grooming, walking, and training the family pet.

The Cocker and the New Baby

Reports of attacks on infants by family dogs have led some people to give up their devoted pets when a new baby arrives. This is truly a shame, for cockers are at their best when they have children to play with. Moreover, animal behavior experts who have studied this problem have concluded that most dogs will not be aggressive toward infants. Dogs that are aggressive toward people, or that tend to chase and attack small animals, however, should never be left unsupervised with an infant.

If you are expecting an addition to your household, there are several precautions you can take to make sure your cocker will accept the new baby. Train the dog to sit or lie down for long periods of time before the baby is born. As you increase the time, accustom your dog to the activities it can expect to see once the baby arrives. Use a doll to imitate carrying, feeding, changing, and bathing the newborn. Remember to praise and reward your dog if it stays still and does not attempt to follow or interfere.

After the birth of the infant, but before bringing him or her home, give your cocker something the baby has used in the hospital, such as a blanket or towel, so that it can become familiar with the little one's scent. Upon returning from the hospital, have the mother greet the dog without the baby. Then place the baby in the nursery, and deny the dog access by using a screen door or folding gate. In this way the dog can see and hear the infant and get used to its presence before the two actually meet.

When the meeting finally occurs, one person should control and praise the dog while another holds the baby. Have the dog sit, and show it the baby. They can remain together for as long as the dog stays calm. In the following weeks you can gradually increase the length of the dog's visit.

While you should never allow the two to be together unsupervised, you must be sure to include your dog in as many activities involving the baby as possible. Your cocker should never feel neglected. By exercising sensitivity to your pet's feelings, you will create an even stronger bond between your cocker and your child.

The Cocker and Other Pets

While cockers usually get along well with other dogs, you should be careful not to let your pet play freely with other smaller animals such as birds or hamsters. After all, the cocker is a hunting dog. Cats, on the other hand, should be dealt with on an individual basis. I have seen cockers and cats that got along like best friends, and I have seen some that were worst enemies.

If you own two cockers, they will enjoy each other's companionship and you should rarely have trouble. Just remember to divide your attention between them evenly. If you do decide to get a second dog, be aware that you will need additional equipment, including another sleeping box or cage and other food dishes.

It is important that your puppy become acquainted with other dogs, and other people as well. Your cocker must become used to crowds and the noises of traffic. Likewise, it must learn how to interact with others of its own kind, a lession that can be learned only if your precious pet is allowed to romp and play with other dogs. If you become overprotective of your cocker and hardly ever let it off the leash, it will not have the freedom to meet and familiarize itself with other dogs and consequently may develop an almost neurotic attitude toward them. It is not at all strange for a cocker to be wary of anything that makes its master anxious. As a result, a cocker that is inexperienced in meeting other dogs may act abnormally when an encounter is forced upon it. It many cases this abnormal behavior confuses the other dog and may lead to biting or even vicious fighting.

Therefore, make it a habit to walk your cocker in areas, such as a park, where it is bound to come into contact with other dogs. When you see another dog,

restrain your cocker until the stranger approaches. Once the two are close, remove the leash from your cocker's collar. A dog kept on a leash tends to be a little bolder and more aggressive because it feels protected by your presence, and thus may be more inclined to fight. Dog etiquette dictates that the two dogs sniff nose to nose. Once familiarity is established, each will then sniff the other's tail or rump. This action usually determines whether they will tolerate each other or become enemies.

In most cases, the two dogs will begin to wag their tails and show the ritualistic signs of friendship. Should you observe other signs, however, such as the hairs on the dogs' necks and backs standing on end, chances are that the animals will attempt to establish a ranking order and perhaps will even fight. At first each dog, in response to its instinct, will attempt to show dominance over the other, perhaps by trying to impress or intimidate the stranger. Dogs exhibiting intimidating behavior will attempt to make themselves look as large as possible by standing every hair on end, tensing their bodies, and taking an arrogant stance. Usually the contestant that achieves the larger appearance will win the higher ranking. If one dog lowers its head, tucks in its tail, and retreats, it has accepted the other dog as dominant and all will be well. If, however, neither backs down, then a growling exhibition or a fight may occur.

In most cases these fights look and sound much worse then they are. Ordinarily, as soon as one of the contestants turns its back and offers an unprotected throat to the other, the fight will end, for along with the instinct to establish ranking order, dogs are equipped with a hereditary behavior pattern that prevents them from biting a dog which acts submissively. Be warned, however, that dogs with behavior problems caused by poor breeding practices may not adhere to the rules of etiquette and may attempt to continue fighting and biting a dog that has shown submission.

Never try to physically separate fighting dogs, for you can easily be bitten. Instead, try to distract them by jumping and yelling or by clapping your hands. Once the dogs are separated, return your dog to its leash and remove it to an area of safety.

The Cocker and Its Master

Although owning a cocker spaniel is a responsibility that entails work, time, and energy, it is also a life-enriching experience. If you provide your cocker with the training it needs and maintain its health and appearance, you will be rewarded many times over with companionship, fun, loyalty, and devotion. The work, time, and energy you put into raising the best dog possible will result in a healthy, long-standing relationship between you and your faithful companion.

But dogs are more than valued companions, hunters, and friends. They inhabit a place deep within us. They occupy our dreams and stimulate our imaginations. Your cocker will fulfill some of your strongest psychic and spiritual needs. Researchers have only begun to examine the psychological benefits of owning and caring for a pet. Companion animals have been shown to reduce stress in their masters and are now being used for their therapeutic effect on the elderly, as well as the physically and mentally handicapped. The simplicity of a dog's behavior can keep us in touch with reality. Dogs are warm, affectionate, and extremely stable—never complex or capricious. They can help people overcome anxiety, grief, depression, loneliness, and pain.

In truth, the cocker can play an important role in the lives of people of any background, status, or life-style. The dog will give you, its master, the unconditional love that you need. The long-term commitment you make to your pet will be rewarded by the emotional security of knowing that, no matter how bad a day you have had, when you eventually return home, your cocker will make you feel loved and appreciated.

Useful Books and Addresses

Books

In addition to the most recent edition of the official publication of the AKC, *The Complete Dog Book*, published by Howell Book House, Inc., in New York, the following publications contain useful information:

Alderton, David. *The Dog Care Manual*. Hauppauge, New York: Barron's Educational Series, Inc., 1986.

Baer, Ted. *Communicating with Your Dog*. Hauppauge, New York: Barron's Educational Series, Inc., 1989.

————*How to Teach Your Old Dog New Tricks*. Hauppauge, New York: Barron's Educational Series, Inc., 1991.

Frye, Fredric. *First Aid for Your Dog*. Hauppauge, New York: Barron's Educational Series, Inc., 1987.

Klever, Ulrich. *The Complete Book of Dog Care*. Hauppauge, New York: Barron's Educational Series, Inc., 1989.

Lorenz, Konrad. *Man Meets Dog*. London and New York: Penguin Books, 1967.

Pinney, Christopher. *Guide to Home Pet Grooming*. Hauppauge, New York: Barron's Educational Series, Inc., 1990.

Smythe, Reginald H. *The Mind of the Dog*. London: Thomas, Bannerstone House, 1961.

Ullman, Hans-J., and Evamaria Ullmann. *The New Dog Handbook*. Hauppauge, New York: Barron's Educational Series, Inc., 1985.

————*Spaniels*. Hauppauge, New York: Barron's Educational Series, Inc., 1982.

Addresses

International Kennel Clubs

American Spaniel Club*
  Mrs. Margaret Ciezkowski, Secretary
  846 Old Stevens Creek Road
  Martinez, GA 30907

American Kennel Club
  51 Madison Avenue
  New York, NY 10038

Australian National Kennel Club
  Royal Show Grounds
  Ascot Vale
  Victoria
  Australia

Canadian Kennel Club
  111 Eglington Avenue
  Toronto 12, Ontario
  Canada

Irish Kennel Club
  41 Harcourt Street
  Dublin 2
  Ireland

The Kennel Club
  1-4 Clargis Street
  Picadilly
  London W7Y 8AB

New Zealand Kennel Club
  P.O. Box 523
  Wellington
  New Zealand

*This address may change as new officers are elected. The latest listing can be obtained from the American Kennel Club.

Index

Index